GARDENING
WITH
COLOR

GARDENING
WITH
COLOR

LANCE HATTATT

This is a Parragon Publishing Book
This edition published in 2003

Parragon Publishing
Queen Street House
4 Queen Street
Bath BA1 1HE, UK

Conceived, edited, illustrated
and produced by Robert Ditchfield Publishers

ISBN 0-75255-740-8

A copy of the British Library Cataloguing in Publication
Data is available from the Library.

Typeset by Action Typesetting Ltd, Gloucester
Color origination by Colour Quest Graphic Services Ltd,
London E9
Printed and bound in China

Half Title: A bright late summer display of Rudbeckia.

Frontispiece: Helenium 'Moerheim Beauty' in dazzling
combination with *Allium spaerocephalon.*

Title Page: Clematis viticella 'Purpurea Plena Elegans'

Opposite: A subtle early summer combination of *Allium
christophii* against a background of purple cotinus and blue
Campanula latiloba.

THE AIM of this book is to provide the gardener with a tool to help him or her plan color schemes in the garden.

Color effects We respond differently to each color and to combinations of color. This book explains the effect of individual colors within a scheme.

Color succession This book provides a wide range of plants through the seasons, with special sections on fall and winter subjects.

SYMBOLS

Where measurements are given, the first is the plant's height followed by its spread. The following symbols are also used in this book:

◐ = thrives best or only in full sun
◑ = thrives best or only in part-shade
● = succeeds in full shade
E = evergreen

Where no sun symbol and no reference to sun or shade is made in the text, it can be assumed that the plant tolerates sun or light shade.

Many plants are poisonous and it must be assumed that no part of a plant should be eaten unless it is known that it is edible.

Contents

Right: A pastel combination for early summer – pale purple dictamnus set against *Rosa* 'Iceberg'.

GARDENING WITH COLOR

The arrangement of color in the garden has to be one of the most satisfying and pleasurable of all the aspects of gardening. It is in this area, more than most, that the gardener is able to find real expression, working with plants to create a living picture which will not only be aesthetically pleasing to others but which will be a fulfilment of a very personal, and often frustrating, striving. For unlike the painter who controls the colors of the palette, the gardener must for ever be subject to the variables of the weather, the caprice of the seasons and the complexity of the plants themselves. But it is in these very challenges that the thrill and excitement of working with color are to be found.

WHY COLOR MATTERS

So much time outdoors seems to be taken up with the seasonal tasks of endless weeding, pruning, deadheading, cutting grass, trimming edges, potting on, and similar mundane chores, that the placing of plants with regard to the maximum effect takes on a secondary role. If this is allowed to happen at all times, then one of the principal joys of the garden will be lost. Each one of us in visiting a garden, or in looking critically at our own, is aware first and foremost of the ways in which color is used to heighten, complement or add to the design.

Gardeners, like artists, have always had a deep interest in color and its effect in a garden setting. Gardeners like Gertrude Jekyll who made public her own innovative ideas on the use of color in books like 'Color in the Flower Garden' as well as articles such as 'Color Effects in the Late Summer Border', have done much to influence the way in which we now think about these matters. Similarly the concept of the color enclosure, the most famous of which is the white garden at Sissinghurst Castle created by Vita Sackville-West in the immediate post-war years, is something which has become firmly rooted in gardening tradition. Looking ahead to the future we see the highly original and bold use of color arranged in

Broad sweeps of color are used in this border.

Drifts of blue forget-me-nots and yellow poppies in a color themed border.

White dominates this springtime planting.

massive drifts of a single plant currently being undertaken in America as well as in a number of European countries.

COLOR EFFECTS

Planning color in any garden is something which is totally individual, a matter of personal taste. Sometimes it is the work of a single person, more often than not it is a shared occupation. Always it is a case of one preference over another.

White gardens, or white borders, have, rather sadly, been over-done, resulting in a plethora of pale imitations of those which are generally regarded as being among the best. Now perhaps is the time to move on, to experiment with more original combinations where white, whilst

remaining the dominant color, is used to contrast or to highlight other shades. For example, those who seek the reassurance of a cool, restful scheme may like to try marrying white with grey and silver. To this could be added, if desired, some of the cool blues. White with lemon, or a stronger gold, works well as does white against green. Whatever, there is room for movement away from the tried and tested schemes of the past towards something new, exciting and different.

Green is very much the color of formality. Tightly clipped yew hedges, neatly arranged box-lined paths, topiary shapes together with carefully formulated foliage effects are all to be found in formal situations. Exceedingly small gardens, such as

Here box provides formality.

Brick paths are marked with shaped domes.

Late summer and this border remains full of color.

those to be had in larger towns and cities, lend themselves particularly well to this kind of treatment. Generally speaking, the smaller the area the more restricted should be the use of color if a co-ordinated, harmonious effect is to be achieved.

Where a garden lends itself to division into outdoor rooms or enclosures, and these do not have to be of any great size, then much enjoyment may be had from creating a themed area which deliberately sets out to convey a particular atmosphere or mood. Colors for something along

these lines will be very much a matter of individual taste, although some consideration should be given to what lies within the immediate surroundings. It would, of course, be a mistake to devise some scheme which upon completion would sit uneasily in its environment. Purples, mauves and blacks may be employed very successfully for a sombre, even melancholy effect, if that is what appeals. Certainly there are to be found some thought-provoking, Gothic gardens which make extensive use of these colors. On a brighter note, late summer herbaceous perennials may be gathered together into a hot garden, of strong reds and yellows, which will themselves suggest climates far removed from our own.

It would be totally wrong to indicate that success, or pleasing results, may only be had where shades of a single color, or colors which work in harmony together, are used. There are many for whom massed floral displays, such as are to be found in public parks or, indeed, to decorate road schemes in urban areas, are a constant source of delight for their very brightness and cheerfulness. There is nothing at all wrong with using color in this manner, although it has to be said that when applied to a domestic situation, then unless great care is taken the results can appear restless and confusing.

GARDENING WITH COLOR

Very often it may prove necessary to alter the garden physically in order to execute a planned color scheme. This may be as little as changing the shape of a border or constructing or planting a new division to form a background. On the other hand it may be far more radical like disposing of some existing feature to bring about a complete change to accommodate some new found interest.

Roses and clematis work together.

Some plants, and thus some color effects, demand certain treatment. For those who carry a love for alpines, then it is first hand knowledge that these little jewels would be lost if left to their own devices in the main borders. To be really effective, and to give of their best, they need to be placed in such a way as to resemble as closely as possible their natural habitat. Devising such a situation, and then arranging them in pleasing color groups to extend over as long a season as possible, is but just one of the ways in which color is used in a practical manner. Roses, possibly more than any other shrubs, lend themselves to being grouped together. The continued popularity of the rose garden is evidence of this. Sadly, all too often, these gardens turn out to be little more than a nightmare of clashing colors where little, if any, thought has been given to the overall effect. This is such a pity for roses are ideal candidates to be partnered with all manner of wonderful complementary plantings.

Not many of us are fortunate enough to possess a wood. In early spring, when the canopy of leaves is down, early flowering treasures, such as the winter aconites, wild daffodils and primroses, could all be employed to provide a succession of color based on a particular theme. Later the scheme could be varied, not only to maintain interest but to allow for later flowering shrubs and perennials.

A sunny site, which may not in itself be very large, could provide a splendid position in which to establish a tapestry carpet of thyme. These low-growing, perennial herbs, flowering over a long period, may be planted out, rather in the manner of a needlework picture, to satisfy with a rich array of color. Depending on the plants chosen, the effect may be one of bright modernity or of faded antique. Full sun, and some shelter,

A skilfully arranged display.

may be the right conditions for growing many of the highly desirable, slightly tender perennials which are so much admired.

SEASONAL COLOR

Each one of the four seasons, around which all gardening revolves, dictates to a certain extent its own colors. Springtime suggests in the main yellow, from the palest of lemons to the deepest of buttery shades. Most likely this is on account of the primroses of the hedgerow and the wealth of cheery daffodils which contribute so much pleasure in town and country gardens alike. But it is also the color of catkins, of witch hazels

Flaming reds, oranges and yellows glow in a woodland area.

and, of course, of the flowers of the forsythia, a shrub which remains as popular as ever. As spring moves into summer, so pastel shades come into their own. Lilacs and roses, irises, campanulas, pale forms of oriental poppy, hardy cranesbill, alliums, lupins and delphiniums, the list is almost endless. Later it is the hot colors which seem to dominate, maybe in preparation for the fall which lies just around the corner.

As the year draws to a close so splendid fall foliage trails a blaze of fire throughout the countryside. Burnished leaves drifting through borders and piling into windswept corners possess their own particular charm. And whilst all of this, sadly, heralds the year's end, it is, not least because of the spectacular color, both thrilling and exciting. Winter is not without considerable color interest. Evergreens make a particularly valuable contribution for it is now, free of other border distractions, that they make their mark most clearly on the landscape. Deciduous trees and shrubs do not deserve to be overlooked. Bare branches and stems, etched against a winter sky, can look breathtakingly wonderful, particularly when dusted with hoar frost. Even the dying leaves of spent perennials add character to the garden in winter.

The Color Wheel

Traditionally the color wheel is made up of three primary colors, red, yellow and blue. By combining these together in equal quantity binary colors, or orange, green and violet, are produced. From mixing one or more of these all other colors are obtained. Colors on the wheel, as illustrated, divide into warm and cool areas. On the warm, or hot, side are red, orange and yellow, although it has to be admitted that lemon yellows cannot be considered hot. The remaining three colors, green, blue and violet, fall onto the cool side.

The hot side of the color wheel.

Amongst the cool colors.

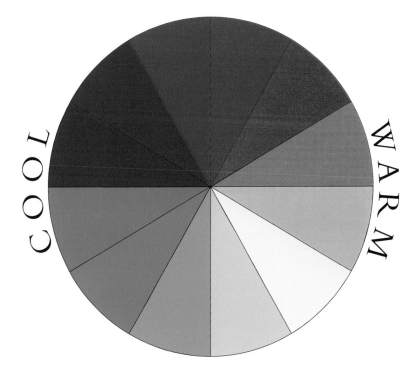

Those colors which are positioned next to each other and which have a pigment in common are said to be in harmony. For example, red and orange, yellow and green, blue and violet, these all harmonize together. Colors which appear opposite to each other on the color wheel, often known as complementary colors, work together too. Red and green, yellow and violet, blue and orange will all complement each other although sometimes the contrast is not to everyone's taste. As a general rule, those colors which do not go together, or which do not appeal on an individual level, may be separated one from the other with the addition of white or grey.

A strong contrast of pansies and tulips. Deep purple as a foil to yellow.

Spires of yellow against soft pink. *Isoplexis sceptrum* and *Verbascum* 'Helen Johnson'.

Pink and blue never fails to delight. Here *Clematis montana* 'Tetrarose' weaves its way through *Ceanothus* 'Puget Blue'.

The main disadvantage of the color wheel is, of course, that it does not take into account all the varying tints in the garden. There are few violet flowers, and fewer red ones, when compared with the vast array of pink ones. Flower color too may be considerably altered by the shape of the actual bloom as well as by texture, so that a mop-headed blossom is likely to deepen a shade whilst an ethereal, airy one will have the opposite effect. However, color is all about individual taste and there are not, nor should there be, any hard and fast rules.

Why Color Varies

Color in nature is subject to so very many forces beyond the control of the individual that at times it would appear as if all success is a matter of chance.

Most difficult to combat is the effect of the weather. Brilliant hot sunshine can alter the appearance of color in the garden just as much as intense cold or strong winds. Rain is by no means a neutral agent. The soft, refreshing showers of early spring serve, particularly when linked to warm sunlight, to heighten and intensify colors. This in direct contrast to fall days of solid rain when everything, seen under lowering, grey skies, becomes almost monochromatic.

Light levels alter as the seasons change. These in turn bring about alterations in the color of leaves and

Kniphofia 'Sunningdale Yellow' brings a brilliance to a summer border.

Astilbes enhanced by their foliage.

White can be startling.

Fuchsias contribute color in late summer.

A cool, restful scene.

flowers. Even within a single day it is possible to be aware of most noticeable differences in color. The pH factor of the soil, that is to say the degree to which it is acid or alkaline, will also affect color tone as will the color instability to be found inherent in all plants.

The best possible means by which to counter all of these things is to be confident in plant knowledge. The experienced gardener will be sure of the habits, likes and dislikes of his or her plants. The beginner will be enthusiastic and quick to learn.

Winter color with cyclamen and autumn crocuses.

Delphiniums make a statement of summer color.

These soft colors of the early summer are in complete harmony.

A midsummer border where the colors are, in the main, muted.

Using Color in the Garden

Few would deny that one of the principal concerns of gardening is the way in which color is employed throughout the garden. What is perhaps less immediately obvious, and certainly open to debate, are the ways and means by which gardeners consciously utilize color in order to achieve particular effects. These may in themselves be intentionally restful schemes or ones deliberately intended to startle, if not shock. What is certain is that they in no small measure serve to give a garden individuality, making each the personal creation of its owner.

In thinking about color in the garden it is possibly helpful to consider the extent to which it is to become an integral part of all planning. Is a particular color border to be

In this garden the emphasis is clearly on summer color.

Trees make real impact.

Gold and purple with two berberis.

Utterly restrained and totally charming.

The skill of the artist in this color grouping.

Gardens need not be a riot of color.

Quiet colors convey peace.

This simple trough is a mass of spring color.

This display will remain looking good well into the fall.

These sweet peas form a colorful centerpiece.

made in isolation, as a casual element within the garden, or is it to be planned as the main focus of a specific area? Is such a border to be viewed from all sides, as is the case with an island bed, or is it to be seen from one, or maybe two, angles only? Does the design allow for it to stand alone, or should it become paired? If not an island bed, then what is to form the background? All of these are questions which will need to be addressed before thoughts and ideas are finalized and work begins in earnest.

In positioning colors within the garden some account should be taken of external factors. The immediate surroundings are important for they will to a large extent determine how colors will appear. Boundaries, forming a background, will need to be in harmony with colors in adjacent borders. The brick of a house, or the paintwork around the windows, may well become determining influences in deciding what should be placed where. In an enclosed area, particularly where a single color is to be used, what is viewed before and after may have a significant bearing on what plantings are chosen. Experimentation, a major part of the fun of gardening, will lead to what is appropriate and effective in each particular situation.

Colors of the Spectrum

The following pages provide a selection of plants divided into color groups to help you plan schemes. Within each color section, plants are listed chronologically from spring to fall/winter.

Yellow and Cream

Yellow and cream are for many the colors of spring, and these shades are certainly not confined to members of the narcissus family. Flowering shrubs, like the familiar and much planted forsythia, or the less well known Chinese witch hazel, *Hamamelis* × *intermedia* 'Pallida', glow in the early sunlight. But, of course, yellow and cream do not belong to a single season. Whether through flower or on account of foliage used to lighten some gloomy corner, these are shades to enjoy all year long. However, what is true, and is possibly one of the reasons why pure yellow, as opposed to cream, remains somewhat unfashionable as a color, is that it is not always the easiest color to place. At all times it cries out for attention, seemingly advancing from its home in the border to meet and hold the eye. For this very reason it needs to be used with care lest it should upstage its companion plantings. Partially concealed from immediate view, to be happened upon as if by chance, a yellow border, or even a single golden foliaged shrub, may be relied upon to bring gaiety, movement and life to the dreariest of garden areas.

***Hamamelis* × *intermedia* 'Pallida'**
Winter-flowering witch hazel is slow growing. 16 × 20ft/5 × 6m

Narcissus bulbocodium Tiny daffodil in late winter and early spring.
◯, 6 × 8in/15 × 20cm

Primula veris Cowslips are to be found in damp meadows and glades. Equally at home in the garden, they may be used to brighten a spring border with their flowers. 8in/20cm

Primula auricula Pale lemon flowers cover this rockery primula each spring. 6 × 8in/15 × 20cm

Narcissus 'Hawera' An exciting, small flowered daffodil for springtime. 1.5ft/45cm

Caltha palustris Marsh marigolds contribute bold color in spring. ○, 1 × 1.5ft/30 × 45cm

Paeonia mlokosewitschii A spring-flowering perennial. Cultivate in humus-rich soil. 2.5 × 2.5ft/75 × 75cm

Meconopsis cambrica, the Welsh poppy, and *Euphorbia polychroma* are placed together at the base of shrubs in this colorful spring scene. The poppies will seed freely throughout a border.

***Kerria japonica* 'Pleniflora'** A vigorous shrub for spring. 6 × 6ft/2 × 2m

***Rosa xanthina* 'Canary Bird'** Of all shrub roses this is one of the earliest to flower. 7 × 7ft/2.2 × 2.2m

***Erythronium* 'Citronella'** Spring-flowering bulb for well drained soil in partial shade. ◑, 1ft × 8in/30 × 20cm

Rosa **'Frühlingsgold'** Butter-yellow, sweetly perfumed flowers clothe long, arching stems on this shrub rose during the late spring and the early summer. 7 × 6ft/2.2 × 2m

Laburnum × *watereri* **'Vossii'** Laburnum blooms in late spring. All parts are poisonous. 33 × 33ft/10 × 10m

Paeonia delavayi **var.** *ludlowii* Tree peonies are striking shrubs to include in any scheme. 8 × 8ft/2.4 × 2.4

Rhodiola rosea (*Sedum rhodiola*) A perennial for well drained soil in full sun. 8in × 1ft/20 × 30cm

Thermopsis montana As summer approaches this perennial begins to flower. 2.5 × 2.5ft/75 × 75cm

Early summer and this border is alive with interest. Lupins dominate, supported with butter-yellow irises. In the foreground a white achillea catches the eye.

***Tanacetum (Chrysanthemum) parthenium* 'Aureum'** The golden-leafed feverfew, with its aromatic leaves, is a short-lived perennial. 9 × 6in/23 × 15cm

Centaurea macrocephala Knapweed flowers in the early part of summer. 3 × 2ft/1m × 60cm

Cephalaria gigantea Flowers supported on tall stems appear at the start of summer. 6 × 4ft/2 × 1.2m

***Rosa* 'Graham Thomas'** Certainly amongst the most free flowering of English roses. Although the main time is early summer, 'Graham Thomas' will bloom for the entire season. 5 × 5ft/1.5 × 1.5m

***Lilium* 'Mont Blanc'** Summer-flowering lilies prefer their bulbs to be placed in free draining soil. For this reason they are ideal for pot cultivation. 4–6ft/1.2–2m

Inula magnifica An herbaceous perennial for the late summer. Placed at the back of the border these flowers are bound to make an impact. 6 × 3ft/2 × 1m

***Santolina chamaecyparissus* 'Lemon Queen'** A summer-flowering shrub with aromatic leaves and lemon flowers. Cut back hard in the spring to retain the shape. ○, E, 2.5 × 3ft/75cm × 1m

Brassy lysimachia, toning roses and swathes of golden rod in this yellow scheme.

***Kniphofia* 'Little Maid'** This summer poker is perennial. Delay cutting back until spring. 2 × 1.5ft/60 × 45cm

Potentilla fruticosa Shrubby potentillas flower for summer and often well into the fall. 4 × 4ft/1.2 × 1.2m

Genista aetnensis Midsummer and the Mount Etna broom is massed with flowers. 13 × 13ft/4 × 4m

Oenothera 'Fireworks' The flowers of this summer perennial are not easily ignored. This is a front of border plant for a situation where a noticeable color is needed. ○, 1.5 × 1ft/45 × 30cm

A magnificent stand of yellow *Coreopsis verticillata* partnered with the slightly tender, velvety red *Cosmos atrosanguineus*.

Dahlia All of the dahlias prove themselves when late summer color is the order of the day. From 1ft/30cm

Helianthus '**Monarch**' Tall growing perennials to flower at the end of summer. ○, 7 × 3ft/2.1 × 1m

Helenium '**Golden Youth**' Perennials like this add color to borders as the days of summer shorten. Divisions will guarantee free flowering plants. ○, 3 × 2ft/1m × 60cm

***Helianthus* 'Lemon Queen'** All of these daisy-type perennials come into their own in late summer. ○, 7 × 3ft/2.1 × 1m

Oenothera missouriensis A form of the perennial evening primrose. In flower all summer. 8in × 2ft/20 × 60cm

***Rudbeckia fulgida* 'Goldsturm'** Fall color is captured in this late-flowering perennial which will continue to bloom for weeks on end. ○, 2.5 × 1.5ft/75 × 45cm

Euonymus fortunei **'Emerald 'n' Gold'**
Variegation on this small, cheerful shrub is
effective throughout the year. E, 3 × 3ft/
1 × 1m

Ilex aquifolium **'Golden Queen'**
Possibly the most brilliant of all cultivars
of common holly. A male variety.
E, 13 × 10ft/4 × 3m

Elaeagnus pungens **'Dicksonii'** This
versatile shrub is most useful for
providing year-round color.
○, E, 8 × 10ft/2.4 × 3m

Choisya ternata **'Sundance'** This
evergreen shrub carries perfumed white
flowers in the spring. ○, E, 6 × 6ft/
2 × 2m

Mahonia lomariifolia Wonderfully scented flowers in late fall and early winter are a bonus with this shrub. Not totally hardy, it must be given the protection of a sunny wall. E, 10 × 6ft/3 × 2m

CONSIDER ALSO:

SHRUBS:
Rhododendron luteum (late spring)

ANNUALS:
Calendula (marigold)
Hibiscus trionum

PERENNIALS:
Primula florindae (summer)

BULBS:
Crocus chrysanthus 'Cream Beauty' (spring)
Tulipa 'West Point' (late spring)

CLIMBERS:
Hedera helix 'Buttercup' (golden foliage)

Jasminum nudiflorum Winter jasmine may be trained against walls. The flowers appear over winter. 8ft/2.4m

Orange

Poor orange, until recently a much despised color among gardeners. Difficult to position with any certainty of success, this is a shade which has for a long time been relegated to the bottom of the heap. Yet this need not be so. For in banishing orange from a place in the border, there is a danger of ruling out of the garden many very worthy subjects.

Indeed, in today's climate where hot borders, the hotter the better, are not only acceptable but increasingly fashionable, orange is making a come-back. For the spirited, there is a case for clashing colors where one brilliant, vibrant shade is set against another. If nothing else, find a space for one of the wonderful acers, such as *Acer palmatum* 'Osakazuki', whose spectacular fall foliage is more than enough to set the world alight.

Geum 'Borisii' Few flowers share the color of this form of water avens. Throughout spring, and into early summer, this perennial will be alive with a succession of blooms. 1.5 × 1.5ft/45 × 45cm

Papaver orientale Oriental poppies remain among the most reliable of all spring flowering perennials. By midsummer both foliage and flowers will have died down. 3 × 2ft/1m × 60cm

Rosa **'Schoolgirl'** Flowers cover this climbing rose during the early part of the summer. 12ft/3.5m

Rosa **'Iris Webb'** A floribunda rose producing pink blooms, with pale orange. 4 × 3ft/1.2 × 1m

Rosa **'Just Joey'** These blooms of creamy orange enlarge as the weather warms. 2.5 × 2ft/75 × 60cm

Rosa **'Anne Harkness'** Plant this healthy floribunda either singly or as a hedge. 4 × 3ft/1.2 × 1m

Rosa **'Sweet Dream'** Patio and miniature roses like this one need not be confined to the border. Free-flowering, they make excellent subjects for containers where they may be positioned for summer-long color. 1.5ft/45cm

Rosa **'Brown Velvet'** Blooms are set off by foliage making this floribunda a flower arranger's dream. 2.5 × 2ft/75 × 60cm

Rosa **'Alchymist'** Midsummer sees this rose, which climbs, a mass of flowers. 12 × 8ft/3.5 × 2.4m

Digitalis parviflora A perennial foxglove for the first part of summer. For partial shade. 3 × 1ft/1m × 30cm

Hemerocallis 'Stafford' Day lilies are summer-flowering perennials, unfussy about situation. 3 × 1ft/1m × 30cm

Tropaeolum tuberosum 'Ken Aslett' A slightly tender climber which grows from a tuber which should, in cold areas, be lifted over winter. Flowers in summer. O, 5ft/1.5m

Crocosmia masoniorum Still known as montbretia, this late summer perennial is noted for its flowers which hang from arching stems. Easy in both sun or partial shade. 2 × 1ft/60 × 30cm

***Helenium* 'Feuersiegel'** End–of–season flowers for a late summer border. Perennial. 3 × 2ft/1m × 60cm

***Crocosmia* 'Harlequin'** This gaily colored montbretia will brighten fall borders. 2 × 1ft/60 × 30cm

Red

Red, so often thought of as a hot color, is not necessarily so. On its cool side are to be found cerise pinks, shades of burgundy, crimson and deep, velvety maroons. They are reliable shades, holding their color well in sunshine, and which appear jewel-like as the shadows lengthen towards the end of day. They give to the garden a feeling of tradition firmly rooted in an accessible past.

On the other hand, the vermilions and scarlets are to be found firmly among the hot reds. With their fiery brilliance they belong to late summer and fall. Within the border they act as accents, advancing to arrest the eye, to advertise their somewhat strident gaiety. Within a large garden they may easily be accommodated. In a smaller area they should be used wisely and with care.

Camellia japonica **'Rubescens Major'** Camellias are shrubs for color at the start of the year. They require acidic soil although they perform in conditions which are neutral. ◯, E, 10 × 10ft/3 × 3m

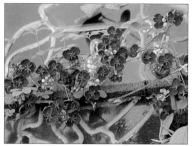

Akebia quinata Slightly tender, the chocolate vine needs sun and protection. Scented flowers in the spring. 30ft/9m

***Tulipa greigii* 'Red Riding Hood'** Bulbs should be set out late fall to flower the following year. 2ft × 8in/60 × 20cm

Rhododendron kaempferi Bursting with flower in the early spring, azaleas make an impact. All azaleas and rhododendrons are best suited to acidic soil and many benefit from leaf-mold.

Tulips like these with their unusual coloring give extra interest to the spring garden.

***Euphorbia griffithii* 'Fireglow'** Orange bracts make this striking for early summer. 3 × 2.5ft/1m × 75cm

Paeonia arietina Peonies are lovely perennials with late spring and early summer flowers. 2.5 × 2ft/75 × 60cm

Rosa moyesii **'Geranium'** Early summer flowers followed in fall with hips.
8 × 7ft/2.4 × 2.2m

Acer palmatum **var. *dissectum* 'Garnet'** Splendid color from beginning to end of the year. 5 × 8ft/1.5 × 2.4m

Tulipa sprengeri Virtually the last tulip to flower, this excites interest as late as early summer. ○, 1.5ft/45cm

Annual poppies bring random color to borders where they seed around. Perennial oriental poppies, flowering at the start of summer, contribute a brief but dazzling show.

Helianthemum **'Supreme'** Rock roses are summer-flowering, for hot, well-drained sites. E, 1 × 3ft/30cm × 1m

Lonicera × *brownii* **'Dropmore Scarlet'** A vigorous climber for midsummer color. 23ft/7m

Clematis **'Niobe'** Velvet flowers of this early summer clematis are especially appealing. This is a climber to grow over a shrub or into the lower branches of a small tree. 10ft/3m

Paeonia lactiflora **'Docteur H. Barnsby'** This peony adds a richness to the summer border. 2 × 2ft/60 × 60cm

Clematis viticella **'Madame Julia Correvon'** This clematis captures attention during late summer. 10ft/3m

Tropaeolum speciosum Midsummer and these brilliant scarlet flowers abound. Position this climber against a dark background. In winter the plant is dormant. 6ft/2m

***Rosa* 'Baron Girod de l'Ain'** Old shrub rose which gives a border needed structure. 5 × 4ft/1.5 × 1.2m

***Rosa* 'Crimson Shower'** Flowers shower this rambling rose against the wall of a house. 20ft/6m

***Rosa* 'Hunter'** One of the rugosa roses which would serve as a hedge within the garden. It would make a background to a border planted in similar shades. ◯, 5 × 5ft/1.5 × 1.5m

Alcea Hollyhocks serve as a reminder of past cottage gardens. 6 × 2ft/2m × 60cm

Fuchsia **'Dollar Princess'** Hardy fuchsias give color from summer to fall. 2.5 × 2.5ft/75 × 75cm

Pelargonium **'Lord Bute'** A summer geranium; overwinter in a frost free greenhouse. ◐, 1.5 × 1.5ft/45 × 45cm

***Penstemon* 'Red Knight'** Penstemons flower, when deadheaded, until the frosts. ○, E, 2.5 × 1.5ft/75 × 45cm

Lychnis chalcedonica These perennials look good in summer when planted in a mass. 3 × 1.5ft/1m × 45cm

***Crocosmia* 'Lucifer'** As summer draws to a close, 'Lucifer' is particularly effective. 4 × 1ft/1.2m × 30cm

Zinnia Sow seed in situ in the late spring in sun. Half-hardy annuals. 2–3ft/60cm–1m

Zauschneria californica Trumpets in later summer earn this perennial a place in a hot border. 2 × 2ft/60 × 60cm

***Dahlia* 'Bishop of Llandaff'** Grown from half-hardy tubers, which must be lifted over the winter, this dahlia is a favorite for the end of summer and into the fall. 3 × 2ft/1m × 60cm

Helenium **'Moerheim Beauty'** Not strictly red as such, this perennial associates perfectly with so many other colors. ○, 3 × 2ft/1m × 60cm

Salvia splendens This tender annual has a place in bedding schemes. ○, 1 × 1ft/ 30 × 30cm

Lobelia 'Compliment' Late summer perennial. Cover in winter. ○, 4 × 1ft/1.2m × 30cm

Tropaeolum majus This scrambling nasturtium is easily raised each year from seed. ○, 1 × 1ft/30 × 30cm

Godetia A hardy annual to liven up the summer borders or to include in pots and containers. Seed of godetia may be bought in mixed packets. 10in–2.5ft/25–75cm

Amaranthus caudatus Love-lies-bleeding is one of the most versatile of all annuals. 4ft/1.2m

***Hibiscus syriacus* 'Woodbridge'** Flowers cover this shrub in late summer. ○, 6 × 6ft/2 × 2m

Fuchsia **'Checkerboard'** Flowers hang in profusion on this eye-catching fuchsia. Use within the border or display in tubs for seasonal color. 2.5 × 2.5ft/75 × 75cm

***Sedum* 'Fall Joy'** Flat heads of flowers remain attractive well into winter. ○, 2 × 2ft/60 × 60cm

Schizostylis coccinea A perennial for moist soil. These flowers appear at the last. 2 × 1ft/60 × 30cm

CONSIDER ALSO:

SHRUBS:
Chaemomeles 'Crimson and Gold' (spring)
Rosa 'Scarlet Fire' (summer)

ANNUALS:
Eschscholzia 'Cherry Ripe'
Papaver commutatum 'Lady Bird'

PERENNIALS:
Dianthus 'Gravetye Gem' (summer)
Iris sibirica 'Helen Astor' (summer)

BULBS:
Anemone fulgens (spring)
Tulipa 'Queen of Sheba' (spring)

***Berberis thunbergii* 'Rose Glow'** The attraction of this easy shrub is the color of the leaves. 5 × 5ft/1.5 × 1.5m

Pinks and Pastels

These are the very essence of the traditional garden with its arbors of old-fashioned roses, paths lined with lavenders, sweetly scented stocks and borders brimming with old-time favorites. All of the lovely pinks, and their associated colors of lilac, pale mauve, washed out purple, rosy red and white streaked with blue, contribute to this.

In early spring, when frosts still play havoc, wonderful camellias come into their own, their dark glossy leaves showing off waxy blooms. Then, too, the daphnes are in flower, their fragrance filling the entire garden. Later the magnolias, cherries in blossom, and early flowering clematis. By summer there are roses, with all their companion plantings, irises, pinks and mallows, lilies and lovely, tender annuals. As warm days ebb away, and the fall approaches, Japanese anemones vie with muted asters to put on a late show.

Camellia ‘Galaxie’ Camellias are shrubs of the early spring. Plant where they thrive in leaf-mould in acidic or neutral soil. ◯, E, 6 × 6ft/2 × 2m

Camellia **'Water Lily'** In spring sugar-pink blooms cover this shrub.
◯, E, 6 × 6ft/2 × 2m

Prunus cerasifera **'Nigra'** Flowers festoon this tree in spring. 15 × 15ft/4.5 × 4.5m

Magnolia × soulangeana **'Lennei'** A spreading tree producing flowers in spring. ◯, 10 × 10ft/3 × 3m

69

Clematis macropetala **'Markham's Pink'** Early flowering climber which can be left to its own devices to weave a passage among other springtime plantings. 6ft/1.8m

Clematis alpina **'Willy'** Seen with *Geranium macrorrhizum*, this climber is a delight in spring. 8ft/2.4m

Clematis **'Nelly Moser'** Flowering in the spring, 'Nelly Moser' never loses popularity. ○, 8ft/2.4m

***Malus* × *moerlandsii* 'Profusion'** Flowering crab-apples are lovely in springtime. Later there will be deep red fruits. 15 × 15ft/4.5 × 4.5m

***Epimedium* × *youngianum* 'Roseum'** Cut foliage back before spring flowers of this perennial emerge. 10in × 1ft/ 25 × 30cm

Scilla non-scripta Pink bluebells make a welcome change in spring. ○, 10in/25cm

71

***Prunus tenella* 'Firehill'** Flowers in spring extend along the branches of this shrub. ○, 6 × 6ft/2 × 2m

***Paeonia suffruticosa* 'Sitifukujin'** This tree peony carries its fine flowers in the spring. ○, 7 × 7ft/2.2 × 2.2m

***Daphne* × *burkwoodii* 'Somerset'** Heavily scented, spring flowering daphnes really do have to be included if at all possible. Slow growing, they are not difficult to accommodate. ○, Semi-E, 5 × 3ft/1.5 × 1m

Paeonia lactiflora **'Monsieur Jules Elie'**
The large, slightly blowzy heads belong to
the early summer. 3 × 3ft/1 × 1m

Incarvillea delavayi This is an early
summer perennial for rich soil in full sun.
○, 2 × 1ft/60 × 30cm

Deutzia × elegantissima **'Rosealind'** Tiny flowers are massed together on this shrub
which blooms from the late spring into the early summer. 3 × 5ft/1 × 1.5m

Tulipa **'China Pink'** Plant bulbs deeply in the fall with a dozen or more to each planting hole. 1.5ft/45cm

Rosa **'May Queen'** Blooms appear on this rambling rose in summer. 15ft/5m

Primula vialii A summer-flowering perennial for moist soil. 1 × 1ft/ 30 × 30cm

Rosa **'Pink Elizabeth Arden'** Furnish large mixed borders at the start of summer with shrub roses such as this one. Feed generously. 5 × 5ft/1.5 × 1.5m

Chaerophyllum hirsutum **'Roseum'** This perennial is like a pink cow parsley. 2 × 2ft/60 × 60cm

Prunella grandiflora **'Pink Loveliness'** Flowers cover this perennial for many weeks in the summertime. 1ft × 1ft/30 × 30cm

Penstemon venustus A penstemon for early summer. Give good drainage and sun. 1.5 × 1.5ft/45 × 45cm

Geranium cinereum **'Ballerina'** A neat plant. After the summer flowers the leaves remain pretty. 8in × 1ft/20 × 30cm

Lathyrus grandiflorus Shades of magenta are to be found in this climbing, everlasting pea. Vigorous, it will put on enough growth in one season to cover a fence. ○, 5ft/1.5m

Clematis viticella **'Margot Koster'** In bloom for the summer, a good climber. 10ft/3m

Papaver rhoeas An annual. This variety is a double form. 1.5ft/45cm

Rosa **'Princess Marie'** Large, rambling roses may be used to climb into trees. 15ft/4.5m

Rosa **'Raubritter'** Clusters of flowers in summer. 3 × 5ft/1 × 1.5

Rosa **'Albertine'** Rambling rose suitable for growing over a pergola. 18ft/5.4m

Oxalis articulata Enjoy these flowers from the late spring onwards. A low growing, easily cultivated perennial which will tolerate dry shade. 8 × 8in/20 × 20cm

Digitalis × mertonensis Perennial flowers in summer on this foxglove. 3 × 2ft/ 1m × 60cm/

***Phlox paniculata* 'Fairy's Petticoat'** Border phloxes are one of the mainstays of summer. 2.5 × 2ft/75 × 60cm

Hydrangea macrophylla As summer gathers pace, so the large mopheads of the hydrangeas come into their own. Color will always vary according to soil type. Hydrangeas are also ideal subjects for tubs or large containers. 6 × 8ft/2 × 2.4m

***Hydrangea macrophylla* 'Ayesha'** The flowers of this hydrangea are unique for the way in which the petals are curved. For best results choose a place in the garden which is slightly shaded. 3 × 5ft/1 × 1.5m

Lythrum salicaria Purple loosestrife is suited to damp conditions. Easy in sun or part shade. 3 × 1ft/1m × 30cm

***Clematis texensis* 'Princess of Wales'** A late flowering clematis. Hard prune in early spring. 10ft/3m

Echinacea purpurea Perennials to include in the late summer border. 4 × 2ft/ 1.2m × 60cm

Fuchsia **'Garden News'** Hardy fuchsias bring color which continues until frosts. 2 × 2ft/60 × 60cm

Oenothera speciosa **'Pink Petticoats'** A pale pink form of the evening primrose to spread at the front of a border. Preferring a sunny spot, it should flower throughout summer. 6in × 2ft/15 × 60cm

Lobelia × speciosa **hybrid** Rich soil, not allowed to dry out, for this summer perennial. 2.5 × 1.5ft/75 × 45cm

Lilium speciosum **var.** *rubrum* A fragrant Japanese lily which flowers in late summer. 5ft/1.5m

Crinum × powellii A bulb sporting trumpet-shaped flowers. To succeed, plant in a hot position in full sun and in soil which is free-draining. ○, 3 × 2ft/1m × 60cm

Schizostylis coccinea **'Sunrise'** Enjoy these late flowering perennials in the fall. 2 × 1ft/60 × 30cm

Gypsophila **'Rosy Veil'** All gypsophilas are summer perennials. This one forms a low mat. 8in × 1ft/20 × 30cm

Nerine bowdenii These fall flowering bulbs hail from South Africa so are, understandably, in need of a site where they may enjoy as much sunshine as possible. ○, 1.5ft × 8in/45 × 20cm

***Aster novi-belgii* 'Goliath'** Fall Michaelmas daisies bring life to the garden as days shorten. 'Goliath', planted in sun, will reward for several weeks with these pink flowers with their bold yellow centers. ◑, 4 × 1.5ft/1.2m × 45cm

Colchicum speciosum Dwarf flowering bulbs for the fall assist in extending the season. The large basal leaves appear after the flowers in late winter or early spring. ◑, 8 × 8in/20 × 20cm

Cleome spinosa The spider flower is an annual which deserves more widespread cultivation. 3ft/1m

***Verbena* 'Aveyron'** A perennial verbena for end-of-season color. Plants like this need to be massed together. 2 × 1ft/ 60 × 30cm

Arbutus unedo* f. *rubra If your soil is inclined towards the acidic, then try this splendid form of the strawberry tree. Strangely, it flowers in the fall at the same time as its fruits begin to ripen. E, 16 × 16ft/5 × 5m

Physostegia virginiana This late summer perennial is ideal for planting between shrubs where it will spread to form an effective and decorative form of ground cover. Once the flowers are over, the whole plant may be cut down to ground level. 1 × 1ft/ 30 × 30cm

CONSIDER ALSO:

SHRUBS:
Kolkwitzia amabilis 'Pink Cloud' (summer)
Rhododendron yakushimanum (spring)
Viburnum × bodnantense 'Dawn' (fall–winter)

ANNUALS:
Cosmos 'Daydream'

PERENNIALS:
Anemone × hybrida 'Queen Charlotte' (late summer-fall)
Phlox 'Mother of Pearl' (summer-fall)

BULBS:
Anemone blanda 'Pink Star' (spring)
Lilium 'Pink Perfection' (summer)

Amaryllis belladonna Late-flowering perfumed bulb. Plant deeply in a sheltered position. ○, 2.5ft/75cm

Purple and Lilac

Of all colors, these are possibly amongst the most moody, often associated, together with black, as the colors of mourning. However, by widening the range to include some shades of lavender, magenta and the darkest of ruby reds, then some exciting variations are realized.

Bearing in mind the potential for creating totally deadening effects, then purple is most certainly not a color for shade. Where possible such hues are best viewed back-lit, that is to say with the sun shining through them from behind. When this occurs, both foliage and flower adopt a magical quality that surprises as much as it delights. If at all possible, then try to contrive such an area within a much frequented part of the garden. Whatever, avoid placing close to the boundaries of a country garden for this is a color which does not associate well with green fields.

Crocus tommasinianus Early spring color develops with these tiny bulbs. Left undisturbed, they will gradually increase with time. 4in/10cm

Pulsatilla vulgaris Rich purple, spring flowers on this perennial plant. The Pasque flower is suitable either for the rock garden or scree bed, or for the front of the border. 1 × 1ft/30 × 30cm

Fritillaria meleagris A spring bulb which is at home growing in grass. Allow to seed. ○, 10in/25cm

Rhododendron augustinii This shrub is massed each spring with flowers. ○, E, 10 × 10ft/3 × 3m

Aquilegia vulgaris **'Adelaide Addison'**
Allow these spring and early summer
perennials to seed around. ○,
2.5 × 1.5ft/75 × 45cm

Nepeta mussinii Catmints are hardy. Cut
back when the early summer flowers are
over. 1.5 × 2.5ft/45 × 75cm

Tulipa **'Blue Heron'** Flowering in the late spring, this wonderful violet-purple tulip
has crystal-like fringes all around the top of the petals, rather like miniature, frosted
icicles. ○, 2ft/60cm

***Clematis* 'Proteus'** Blooms of a delicate mauve-pink. The main flowering period is in the first part of the summer. However, it will produce a reasonable second show just before the fall. 6ft/2m

Abutilon suntense Late spring onwards sees this shrub in flower. Slightly tender. ◑, 15 × 10ft/5 × 3m

Wisteria floribunda One of the sights of early summer are the long racemes of a well-grown wisteria. ◑, 30ft/9m

Clematis **'Haku-ôkan'** This climber blooms towards the end of spring. 6ft/2m

Within this garden a sunny slope has been used with great imagination and artistry.
Different creeping thymes, with an emphasis on dark purple, have been arranged to
resemble an antique rug thrown carelessly to one side.

Trifolium rubens An unusual perennial
with flower heads in the early summer.
1 × 1ft/30 × 30cm

Malva sylvestris mauritiana Flowers
appear on this perennial from spring until
the fall. ○, 4 × 2ft/1.2m × 60cm

Allium aflatunense **'Purple Sensation'**
Combine this tall-growing bulb with
purple bearded irises for springtime color.
3ft/1m

Iris **'Mandarin'** In this planting it looks
fine in early summer against the
euphorbia. 3 × 1ft/1m × 30cm

Penstemon glaber All of the penstemons will repay dead-heading. To extend the season,
select *Penstemon* 'Papal Purple', 'Blackbird' and 'Catherine de la Mare'.
○, E, 2 × 2ft/60 × 60cm

***Rosa* 'Zigeunerknabe' ('Gipsy Boy')**
Summer-flowering roses are wonderful
shrubs. 5 × 4ft/1.5 × 1.2m

***Rosa* 'Bleu Magenta'** Clusters of blooms
cling to the stems of this climbing rose.
15ft/4.5m

***Rosa* 'Blue Boy'** Place this shrub rose as the centerpiece of a border devoted to
shades of crimson, magenta, deep pink and violet for an exciting and out of the
ordinary picture. 3 × 3ft/1 × 1m

Phlox **'Chattahoochee'** For spring color, plant this perennial phlox in a sunny spot. 8in × 1ft/20 × 30cm

Rosa **'Veilchenblau'** A rose to climb over a pergola or a wall. 12ft/3.5m

Erigeron speciosus **'Pink Jewel'** This lilac-pink daisy with a center of old gold will be in flower each year all through the summer. 2.5 × 1ft/75 × 30cm

Salvia sclarea* var. *turkestanica Faded
purple bracts appear from midsummer on
this biennial sage. 2.5 × 1ft/75 × 30cm

Acanthus spinosissimus A perennial with
flowers in midsummer. ○, 4 × 2.5ft/
1.2 × 75cm

***Clematis viticella* 'Etoile Violette'** Flowers first appear in midsummer and continue well into the fall. Viticella clematis are pruned in the late winter to ground level. 10ft/3m

Aster frikartii **'Mönch'** Summer-flowering Michaelmas daisy. It blooms for months on end. ◯, 2.5 × 1.5ft/75 × 45cm

Verbena bonariensis Grow this short-lived perennial at the front of the border from midsummer onwards. 4ft × 6in/ 1.2m × 15cm

Allium sphaerocephalon Known as the round-headed leek, these bulbs may be used to grow up through other summer plantings. Plant in sufficient numbers to look purposeful. 1–2ft/30–60cm

Passiflora caerulea The common name for this summer climber is the passion flower. It is probably the hardiest. ○, 20ft/6m

Geranium clarkei **'Kashmir Purple'** Perennial hardy geranium. This flowers in summer. 1 × 1ft/30 × 30cm

This section of a late summer border brings together shrubs and perennials of similar tones. Plants featuring here are *Hydrangea aspera* Villosa Group, a border phlox and the flat heads of *Achillea millefolium* 'Lilac Beauty'.

Lavenders possess an old-fashioned quality. As illustrated here, they may be planted together to join up as an informal, but colorful and scented hedge.

***Buddleja davidii* 'Dartmoor'** Flower spikes appear on the current growth of this shrub towards the end of summer. 10 × 10ft/3 × 3m

Gladiolus papilio This is in flower as summer ends. 3ft/1m

Salvia horminum Grow this form of annual clary for its dark violet bracts in summertime. An excellent plant for flower arrangers. 1.5ft/45cm

Eupatorium purpureum A tall perennial for the end of summer. Place in moist soil. 6 × 3ft/2 × 1m

***Clematis viticella* 'Purpurea Plena Elegans'** With double blooms, this is a climber for late summer and early fall. 12ft/3.5m

A fall border at its best. Michaelmas daisies, in shades of pale mauve, lavender and lilac, are grouped together in this garden to give a misty effect.

CONSIDER ALSO:

SHRUBS:
Buddleja davidii
  'Black Knight'
  (late summer)
Syringa 'Elinor'
  (early summer)

ANNUALS:
Heliotropium
  'Marine'
Petunia 'Plum
  Purple'

PERENNIALS:
Geranium
  magnificum
  (summer)
Liriope muscari
  (fall)

BULBS:
Iris reticulata
  (spring)
Tulipa 'First Lady'

***Clematis* 'Gypsy Queen'** Plum-purple flowers appear on this climber from the middle of summer until the fall. 10ft/3m

Blue

Blue remains one of the most covetable of all colors within the garden. Perhaps this is in no small measure because of its shy, retiring habit. Unassertive, it is one of the last colors to declare itself in the early morning and, as the dusk gathers, the first to fade from prominence. Because of this it is useful for creating a sense of distance, for conveying the impression that a border, or indeed garden, is actually rather longer than it in fact is.

Blue used singly may well appear a little dull, lifeless and lack-luster. It is a color to be partnered with others in a deliberately thought out scheme, or to be a token, a mere suggestion, within a mixed color border.

Lithodora diffusa Poor, stony, lime-free soil is the ideal medium in which to grow this shrub which will produce flowers for the greater part of the summer. 1 × 2ft/ 30 × 60cm

Scilla mischtschenkoana Early squills
enjoy a situation not too hot. 4in/10cm

Chionodoxa luciliae Glory of the Snow
bulbs flower at the start of the spring.
4in/10cm

***Clematis* 'Blue Bird'** Choose early spring flowering clematis for color at the start of
the year. All of the alpina types look effective trained to grow through a shrub.
6–8ft/1.8–2.4m

Gentiana acaulis For the spring rock garden. ◑, E, 4 × 6in/10 × 15cm

Corydalis flexuosa Flowers in the springtime. Position in semi-shade. 1 × 1ft/30 × 30cm

Brunnera macrophylla The Siberian bugloss makes excellent ground cover in the spring garden. ◑, 1.5 × 2ft/ 45 × 60cm

Muscari aucheri This grape hyacinth will provide vivid color each spring. 4–6in/10–15cm

Veronica pinnata **'Blue Eyes'** Plant this summer-flowering perennial at the front of a border. ○, 8in × 1ft/20 × 30cm

Veronica teucrium **'Shirley Blue'** This perennial flowers profusely throughout the summer. 8in × 1ft/20 × 30cm

Iris missouriensis This iris will thrive with blooms in early summer. 2 × 2ft/ 60 × 60cm

Iris sibirica **'Soft Blue'** Border plants for the late spring into the first part of summer. 2.5 × 2ft/80 × 60cm

Rosmarinus officinalis Common rosemary need not be confined to the herb garden. ○, E, 5 × 5ft/1.5 × 1.5m

Ceanothus impressus Grow this shrub for its deep blue flowers each springtime. ○, E, 5 × 10ft/1.5 × 3m

Ceanothus **'Blue Mound'** In a small garden, this shrub is ideal. The flowers appear from late spring. All ceanothus benefit from shelter and good drainage. ○, E, 1 × 2ft/30 × 60cm

Camassia leichtlinii Flowers rise out of lush foliage in early summer. 2.5 × 1ft/ 75 × 30cm

Campanula latiloba Spires of blue bring a vibrancy to summer borders. 2 × 2ft/ 60 × 60cm

Delphinium belladonna '**Lamartine**' Perennial delphiniums are one of the mainstays of the garden in the summer. Tall stems, which may require staking, give height to borders. 5 × 2ft/1.5m × 60cm

Felicia amelloides A tender perennial best treated as an annual. Flowers throughout summer. Grow them also in pots and containers. ○, 1.5 × 1.5ft/45 × 45cm

Clematis durandii Flowers from midsummer until the fall. 3–4ft/1–1.2m

Anchusa azurea **'Loddon Royalist'** True blue for the first part of summer. 4 × 2ft/1.2 × 60cm

Campanula latifolia Flowers mass this
perennial in summer. 3 × 2ft/1m × 60cm

Campanula cochleariifolia A mat of bells
in midsummer. 4in × 2ft/10 × 60cm

Salvia patens A summer-flowering
perennial. This is not hardy.
2 × 1.5ft/0 × 45cm

111

***Hydrangea macrophylla* 'Blue Wave'** Late summer flowering shrub. The exact color depends on the soil. The greater the acidity, the more intense the blue. 6 × 9ft/ 2 × 2.7m

Hydrangeas add flamboyancy to end of summer borders.

***Ceanothus* 'Autumnal Blue'** A late summer flowering shrub amongst the hardiest of ceanothus. ○, E, 13 × 13ft/ 4 × 4m

Platycodon grandiflorus mariesii Open panned flowers line the stems of this perennial in summer. The balloon flower will tolerate most situations apart from complete shade. 2 × 1.5ft/60 × 45cm

Allium beesianum One of the onion family, this bulbous plant flowers in summer. 1.5ft/45cm

***Agapanthus* Headbourne Hybrids** Flowerheads in summer. Bulbs are exceedingly hardy. ○, 2 × 1.5ft/ 60 × 45cm

Ceratostigma plumbaginoides The hardy plumbago is one of the loveliest of shrubs for its flowers in early fall. Position where it will catch the sun in dry, well drained soil. 3 × 5ft/1 × 1.5m

Perovskia atriplicifolia Russian sage is a shrub to enjoy in later summer. 3 × 5ft/1 × 1.5m

Nicandra physalodes The shoo-fly, a hardy annual, flowers in late summer. 3–4ft/1–1.2m

Caryopteris* × *clandonensis This small shrub is valued for its late flowers over glaucous leaves. ◗, 2.5 × 2.5ft/80 × 80cm

***Picea pungens* 'Koster'** The leaves of this pine are silvery-blue, spectacular during winter. E, 43 × 26ft/13 × 8m

CONSIDER ALSO:

SHRUBS:
Hibiscus syriacus
'Bluebird' (late
summer)

ANNUALS:
Nigella damascena
(Love-in-a-
mist)
*Phacelia
campanularia*

PERENNIALS:
*Pulmonaria
angustifolia*
'Munstead
Blue' (spring)
Salvia uliginosa
(fall)

BULBS:
Muscari neglectum
(spring)
Scilla sibirica
'Spring Beauty'

Ilex meservae The blue holly takes its name from its blue foliage. E, 10 × 8ft/ 3 × 2.4m

115

Green

Of all the colors in the garden green is, for some extraordinary reason, the least valued. Featuring so often, and in so many guises, its true worth has almost completely become overlooked. Yet green is the most restful of colors which, acting as a foil to others, brings order, harmony and certain restraint to even the most restless of schemes.

That apart, it brings with it wonderful variation of form and texture to be found in both leaf and flower alike. For green encompasses so much. It is the color of so many grasses, of ferns, of sedges and bamboos, of trees and shrubs unfurling new, precious shoots in the early spring as well as the bold sentinels of evergreens dominating the winter landscape. Green flowers give a subtlety to borders for they are understated and often, delightfully, unexpected.

Formal, structured gardens, where flowers may appear inappropriate, depend almost in their entirety on form provided by such plants as clipped box, yew, Portuguese laurel (*Prunus lusitanica*), hollies and ivies as well, of course, as grass with which to set off the whole effect.

This corner of a terrace relies heavily on green plants, both for their form and texture, to create an effect which is restful yet is not without interest.

Garrya elliptica Shrub noted for catkins in winter, best on male plants. E, 13 × 10ft/4 × 3m

Helleborus argutifolius This perennial is a delight in the early year. E, 2 × 3ft/ 60 × 90cm

***Euphorbia characias* ssp. *wulfenii* 'Lambrook Gold'** This fine form of spurge flowers in spring. 4 × 3ft/ 1.2m × 1m

Dark yew sets off these viridiflora tulips, *Tulipa* 'Spring Green'. Combined with these is *Euphorbia polychroma*, its bracts complementing the color of the tulips.

An unusual use of fennel, its foliage contrasted with the eryngium.

This composition is principally made up of *Heuchera* 'Greenfinch', *Iris pseudacorus* and *Rheum alexandrae*.

Smyrnium perfoliatum Yellow-green flowers of this summer perennial give scope to gardeners. 3 × 2ft/1m × 60cm

Euphorbia × martinii A spurge with flower spikes from early summer. ○, 2 × 1ft/60 × 30cm

Bupleurum angulosum A much admired perennial for its flowers. Place in sun. 2 × 1ft/60 × 30cm

Seedheads of crown imperials extend the period of interest of these bulbous plants.

These mixed conifers are highlighted by a broad sweep of lady's mantle which produces lime-green flowers throughout the summer months. *Alchemilla mollis* self-seeds freely. 1.5 × 1.5ft/45 × 45cm

Stipa tenuissima This perennial grass looks pleasing in late summer when it flowers. ○, 2 × 1.5ft/60 × 45cm

Euphorbia sikkimensis A foliage plant with lime bracts for weeks in summer. 3 × 2½ft/1m × 75cm

Nicotiana Green tobacco plants. This annual is not completely hardy. 3 × 1ft/1m × 30cm

Eucomis bicolor A bulb for a warm position. Spires in late summer. ○, 1.5 × 2ft/45 × 60cm

Adiantum venustum Plant the deciduous maidenhair fern to enjoy its delicate foliage. 10 × 10in/25 × 25cm

Polystichum setiferum 'Divisilobum' The shield fern is evergreen. E, 4 × 3ft/ 1.2m × 1m

Veratrum nigrum Leaves of this perennial open out as variegated surfaces. Late summer flowers. 5 × 2ft/1.5m × 60cm

Laurus nobilis Bay may be grown as a handsome, evergreen shrub. ○, 23 × 6ft/7 × 2m

Hebe cupressoides **'Boughton Dome'** This hebe makes up for lack of flowers by being evergreen and shapely. Placed within a border it contributes year-round form. 2.5 × 2.5ft/75 × 75cm

Miscanthus **'Silver Feather'** Glossy green leaves, with variegation, are followed with plumes. 6 × 2ft/2m × 60cm

Pseudosasa japonica Evergreen bamboo, which produces a thicket of canes. 15ft/5m indefinite spread

Phormium tenax The evergreen phormium is dramatic. During cold winters it may prove wise to protect with old sacking. 10 × 3ft/3 × 1m

***Hebe* × *divergens* 'Edinensis'** The architectural quality of this evergreen shrub should not be overlooked. In this picture it has been caught heavily laden with frost.
1 × 3ft/30cm × 1m

Salvia officinalis Evergreen, shrubby sage with its aromatic leaves. For sun.
3 × 3ft/1 × 1m

Tanacetum vulgare The leaves of this tansy make it highly decorative. 3 × 2ft/
1m × 60cm

Variegation

Variegation in plants, usually to be found in foliage, provides an element of variety within the garden and is popular with gardeners very often as a means of brightening some otherwise gloomy or dark corner. Brought about by a chlorophyll deficiency in the main, variegated plants have in recent times been avidly collected by enthusiasts. If there is any danger in this, then it lies in over-planting. Much greater harmony overall will be found where plants with variegation are used sparingly, perhaps singly, or as part of a carefully thought out, color-themed border.

All combinations are inclined from time to time to revert to plain green. Where individual leaves, or even whole stems or branches, do revert, then these should be cut out immediately they are first spotted.

Weigela florida **'Variegata'** This shrub appears fresh on account of its foliage. Arching branches of flowers in early summer make it ideal. 5 × 5ft/1.5 × 1.5

***Euonymus fortunei* 'Silver Queen'** This has crisp leaves which are evergreen. E, 8 × 5ft/2.4 × 1.5m

***Euonymus fortunei* 'Emerald 'n' Gold'** Much of the popularity of this shrub has to be on account of its foliage. E, 3 × 5ft/1 × 1.5m

***Cornus alba* 'Elegantissima'** This red-barked dogwood may be used to lighten a dull spot or as a basis for an all white scheme. 10 × 13ft/3 × 4m

Ilex aquifolium **'Argentea Marginata Pendula'** Hollies are useful for providing out–of–season color. E, 8 × 8ft/2.4 × 2.4m

Leucothoe walteri **'Rainbow'** A shrub with pink, variegated leaves. 2.5 × 3ft/ 75cm × 1m

Aralia elata **'Variegata'** Japanese angelica tree merits a warm situation where new foliage won't be frosted. In late summer it is massed with white flowers. 12 × 10ft/3.5 × 3m

***Aucuba japonica* 'Gold Dust'** Aucubas may be relied upon to thrive in difficult situations. E, 8 × 8ft/2.4 × 2.4m

***Lonicera japonica* 'Aureoreticulata'** The attraction of this honeysuckle is its leaves. 10ft/3m

***Acer negundo* 'Flamingo'** The appeal of this deciduous tree has to be the variegation of the leaves. Distinctly marked white, green and pink they create a display. 26 × 20ft/8 × 6m

Hosta **'Frances Williams'** Lime-green is matched in equal parts with grey-green for an unusual combination. 2.5 × 2.5ft/ 75 × 75cm

Hedera colchica **'Sulphur Heart'** Bold splashes of gold color the vibrant green of this evergreen, climbing ivy. E, 15ft/4.5m

Brunnera macrophylla **'Dawson's White'** In maturity these spring-flowering perennials make an excellent plant. ○, 1.5 × 2ft/45 × 60cm

Hedera helix **'Goldheart'** This evergreen favorite ivy really is alight with color throughout the year. E, 30ft/9m

***Houttuynia cordata* 'Chameleon'** This showy, ground-cover perennial is all too often overlooked as an interesting plant for the garden. It makes a lovely addition to the water garden where it enjoys moisture retentive soil. ☽, 4in/10cm, indefinite spread

***Thymus* 'Doone Valley'** Tiny aromatic flowers and leaves have made thyme an enduring plant. 4in/10cm

***Spartina pectinata* 'Aureomarginata'** Plant close to water with room to spread as it can prove to be invasive. 6ft/1.8m

131

White, Grey and Black

Gardening in this range makes its own demands, but white flowers and grey leaves, for example, are vital components of the plantsman's palette, though black tends to be more of a sought-after oddity.

White

White, the symbol of purity, innocence and perfection continues, more than any other color in the garden, to hold the position of utmost supremacy. White flowers in absolute plenty carry with them a richness married with, paradoxically, a quiet, gentle sophistication.

To be totally successful, white, unless used as a highlight, requires its own space, possibly within some secret and enclosed area where its impact will be absolute and complete. For this a background of formally arranged, clipped yew is ideal. Where this is not a possibility, then a boundary clothed in some dark evergreen, such as ivy, would suffice as well. Within this enclosure light plays an important role. Overhead daylight with the presence of a strong summer sun will do little for the colors beyond reducing them to a uniform drabness. To excel, they must enjoy the benefit of shade.

Probably one of the most famous of all white gardens, this one at Sissinghurst Castle in Kent was created by Vita Sackville-West in the years immediately following the Second World War.

Helleborus niger The Christmas rose brings cheer to the garden in the early part of the year. Plant in a slightly shaded situation. E, ○, 1.5 × 1.5ft/45 × 45cm

***Narcissus* 'Flower Drift'** Many of the white flowered daffodils would be most suitable for a pale scheme. 1.5 × 1.5ft/ 45 × 45cm

***Camellia japonica* 'Nobilissima'** The pure white flowerhead of this early camellia is particularly enticing. E, 10 × 6ft/3 × 2m

Syringa vulgaris A white form of the common lilac for spring color. A hardy shrub. 20 × 13ft/6 × 4m

Erythronium californicum '**White Beauty**' Erythroniums are especially attractive spring bulbs for a lightly shaded area. ◑, 1ft × 8in/30 × 20cm

Tulipa '**Purissima**' Spring-flowering bulbs are a must in any garden. 16 × 8in/40 × 20cm

Anemone blanda '**White Splendour**' Scatter these tiny bulbs beneath shrubs to enjoy flowers in the spring. 4in/10cm

Prunus 'Tai Haku' The Great White Cherry is spectacular in flower. 26 × 26ft/ 8 × 8m

Viburnum plicatum 'Mariesii' Flat white flower corymbs in the late spring and first part of the summer. 10 × 13ft/3 × 4m

Geranium macrorrhizum 'Album' A spreading, hardy perennial to use as ground cover under and around trees and shrubs. 2 × 2ft/60 × 60cm

Tiarella cordifolia Feathery white racemes appear from the late spring well into early summer. 1 × 1ft/30 × 30cm

Libertia formosa Flowers throughout spring. A hardy perennial. Semi-E, 3 × 3ft/1 × 1m

Wisteria floribunda **'Alba'** Wisteria is grown for its long flower racemes in early summer. ○, 30ft/9m

Cistus **'Paladin'** A shrub for a hot, dry, sunny site. Paper-white flower petals are blotched a deep wine red and are carried over glossy, dark green leaves. ○, E, 6 × 6ft/2 × 2m

Centranthus ruber albus Perennial valerian is likely to seed around. Continuous color from early summer. 3 × 1.5ft/ 1m × 45cm

Sidalcea candida A flowering period from early summer until the fall from this herbaceous perennial. 3 × 2.5ft/ 1m × 75cm

A lovely grouping of perennials. Note how seedlings are permitted, adding to the relaxed atmosphere. Included are *Lychnis coronaria* 'Alba', astrantia and poppies.

Iris orientalis A perennial iris flowering in the late spring and early summer. 2 × 2ft/60 × 60cm

Nicotiana The fragrant tobacco plant is most usually grown as an annual. Plant in sun. 1ft × 6in/30 × 15cm

Rosa **'Iceberg'** Early summer is the time for roses. Of all the floribunda roses 'Iceberg' retains its popularity. These blooms, which appear for an extended season, sustain color in an all white garden. 4 × 4ft/1.2 × 1.2m

Lilium regale Summer-flowering lilies, deeply scented, are one of the joys of the garden. This one is no exception. Seen here, it is planted in a border where, given good drainage, the bulbs will flower for many years. 4ft/1.2m

Lilium **'Olivia'** Bulbous lilies may be successfully grown in pots. 4ft/1.2m

Campanula latiloba alba Summer-flowering, this is a perennial for any white garden. 4 × 1ft/1.2m × 30cm

Campanula persicifolia The white form of this perennial, in midsummer, is emphasized by the blue. ◑, 3 × 1ft/ 1m × 30cm

***Clematis viticella* 'Little Nell'** This late summer viticella is white with pink. 10–12ft/3–3.6m

Leucanthemum × superbum Shasta daisies are tough perennials with which to fill late summer borders. 4 × 3ft/1.2 × 1m

Malva moschata alba An easy perennial which will spread in most normal garden soils. 2 × 2ft/60 × 60cm

An ethereal quality is achieved in a large border. Tall spires of *Veronicastrum virginicum* provide a backdrop to the paper-like flowers of *Anaphalis margaritacea*.

Anemone* × *hybrida Japanese anemones must be amongst the most accommodating of all garden plants. Perennial and hardy, they cover the ground and flower for weeks from late summer onwards. 5 × 2ft/1.5m × 60cm

***Echinacea purpurea* 'White Swan'** One of the most admired of all late summer perennials on account of its green tinted petals and centre. Cone flowers will thrive in most garden soils. 4 × 2.5ft/1.2m × 75cm

Artemisia lactiflora **Guizhou Group**
Airy flowers on this perennial which is
suited to the front of the border as to the
rear. 3 × 2ft/1m × 60cm

Cosmos Include annual white cosmos in
summer bedding schemes. Prefers sun.
2ft/60cm

Crinum × *powellii* **'Album'** Bulbs of late summer crinums prefer to be planted in a
sheltered position, possibly against a wall and to be given free draining soil.
○, 3 × 2ft/1m × 60cm

Magnolia grandiflora This slow growing variety blooms at the end of summer. Best in shelter. ◯, E, 33 × 33ft/10 × 10m

Dahlia Dahlias are not frost hardy. Most flower at the year's end. From 1ft/30cm

Gladiolus These flowers for summer come from corms which must be lifted at the first frosts. ◯, 4 × 1ft/1.2m × 30cm

Cimicifuga simplex A late flowering perennial producing spikes well into the fall. 3 × 2ft/1m × 60cm

Colchicum fallale **'Album'** These are fall-flowering bulbs to naturalize in grass.
8 × 8in/20 × 20cm

CONSIDER ALSO:

SHRUBS:
*Carpenteria
 californica*
 (summer)
Magnolia stellata
 'Royal Star'
 (spring)
Romneya coulteri
 (sum–aut)
ANNUALS:
*Argemone
 grandiflora*

PERENNIALS:
Astilbe
 'Deutschland'
 (summer)
*Pulmonaria
 officinalis*
 'Sissinghurst
 White' (spring)
BULBS:
Crocus chrysanthus
 'Snow Bunting'
 (early spring)

Cyclamen hederifolium **f.** *album* These little bulbs are fall-flowering. Leaves are attractive. Following immediately after the flowers, they are ivy-shaped of silvery green. 4 × 8in/10 × 20cm

Cortaderia selloana The pampas grass at the end of the year. Cut back hard to the ground each spring but wear gloves as the leaves are sharp. 6 × 4ft/2 × 1.2m

Grey

First and foremost, grey is invaluable for separating colors which do not combine well together and which result in the most horrible of clashes.

Second, rather in the manner of white, grey helps to shape a border, to give it visual balance and form.

But, more than anything else, grey is such a wonderful partner to other plants. For a really moody, even gothic, effect, then combine it with deep purple or darkest magenta. Where a soft, dreamy picture is appropriate, then place it among pinks, lemons, lavenders and greens. For something much more startling and daring, mix grey with the lacquer red of a Chinese bridge or position it with the brown of a Russian bear. And, most difficult of all, use grey with black. The results are stunning!

Here grey is seen at its most architectural. The onopordum is deliberately chosen to tower over the alliums to give a sense of drama to this border which has been formally edged with box.

Ghost-grey leaves of the curry plant, *Helichrysum italicum*, appear to float over the grey-green rue, *Ruta graveolens*.

Stachys byzantina has been imaginatively used here to highlight the purple foliage of *Lysimachia ciliata* 'Firecracker'.

Grey shrubs and perennials help to create depth and space in a border. Placed with care they may also either highlight other plantings or, indeed, tone down those which may approach the garish.

Blue and grey successfully combine together, as illustrated here, to make for a cool interlude within a planting scheme. Not only do the mid-blues look well with grey, but also those which are darker.

Verbascum olympicum Mulleins are surely amongst the loveliest of perennials. 6 × 2ft/2m × 60cm

Scotch thistles have been positioned with the spike-forming fox-tail lily, *Eremurus stenophyllus* ssp. *stenophyllus*.

Through the deep, plum-colored leaves of the *Heuchera micrantha* 'Palace Purple' the finely cut foliage of the silvery *Artemisia* 'Powis Castle' appears to weave a magical spell.

This anaphalis, shown in the foreground, brings a certain unity to the other colors in the border.

Fine grey foliage, such as is to be found on this tanacetum, is best when seen in contrast.

At the base of the burgundy cotinus a broad band of silver-leafed artemisia strikes a forceful contrast. The cotinus may be hard pruned each spring to promote new, richly colored growth.

Scale in the garden is important. A low wall of the compact shrub, *Berberis thunbergii* 'Bagatelle', is shown off by the non-flowering, *Stachys byzantina* 'Silver Carpet'.

Tall growing stachys amongst other varied colors. In this way the eye is given rest.

Cineraria, with grey leaves, has been included, like a mark of punctuation in a sentence.

The cool, yet dramatic effect of grey *Artemisia ludoviciana* 'Valerie Finnis', white achillea and a note of acid green introduced in the foliage of *Achillea grandifolia*.

Eryngium* × *zabelii Crowding the front of the border are these summer-flowering perennial plants with their flower heads, ideal for the flower arranger either fresh or dried. ○, 1.5ft × 10in/45 × 25cm

Silver-grey artemisia acts as a screen, turning yellow anthemis gold.

Tanacetum haradjanii This tansy is grown for foliage. Contrast it with any dark flower. ○, 2 × 2ft/60 × 60cm

Here anaphalis is a backdrop to summer-flowering border phlox. All greys associate well with pink to mauve and may be used as underplanting and ground cover.

CONSIDER ALSO:	
SHRUBS AND	*Eucalyptus gunnii*
TREES:	*Pyrus salicifolia*
Ballota	'Pendula'

***Brachyglottis* (*Senecio*) 'Sunshine'** This shrub in summer is covered in yellow flowers. ◖, E, 3 × 5ft/1 × 1.5m

Black

Black as a color within the garden must, inevitably, be limited to flowers of the darkest hue, to foliage of a similar nature and to the stems of many shrubs and trees, most apparent in wintertime. A really black grass, however, does exist, *Ophiopogon planiscapus* 'Nigrescens', sometimes known as Black Dragon, which is most effective in a mass.

The impact of black in the garden must lie in the way in which it is combined with other plants to create a sense of mystery, or to be used for dramatic effect.

Tulipa **'Queen of Night'** looks striking against silver-grey *Cynara cardunculus*. 1.5ft/45cm

Tulipa **'Black Parrot'** Plant in large groups for best results as tulips, and these are no exception, are so much better in a mass. Try them too in containers to be taken indoors at flowering time. 1.5ft/45cm

***Aquilegia vulgaris* 'Magpie'** Columbines remain a perennial favorite for the early summer border. Plant with dark purples. 3 × 1.5ft/1m × 45cm

***Viola* 'Bowles' Black'** Grown at the base of a yew hedge they will reinforce a somber look. 4in × 1ft/10 × 30cm

Helleborus orientalis Hellebores with their evergreen foliage, are wonderful perennial plants for the spring. ◑, E, 1.5 × 1.5ft/45 × 45cm

***Ophiopogon planiscapus* 'Nigrescens'** This perennial grass is able to look effective with so many other plants. 10 × 10in/25 × 25cm

Color
Combinations

The color of one flower affects our perception of the color of the flower next to it. Some of the most successful color combinations are shown on the following pages.

Yellow with White

Soft, pale yellows are the colors of springtime and early summer. Not for now the strong golds of late summer and fall, but gentle tints which suggest rather than state. Teamed with white they take on a lightness of tone.

Such a combination is seldom commonplace. It remains both subtle and suggestive, an understatement, demanding of close observation. Enjoy them particularly in the evening as the light fades when they will take on a luminosity which is, at times, unforgettable.

Spires of verbascum glow in this summer scheme. Intermingling are feverfew, *Tanacetum parthenium*.

Rosa 'Canary Bird' and *Veronica gentianoides* 'Tissington White' are the principal players in this yellow and white spring border. Creamy *Aquilegia* 'Edelweiss' provides a link between the two.

Wonderfully warm, butter-yellow heads of *Tulipa* 'Maréchal Niel' crown a carpet of white Universal pansies in this highly imaginative and very successful scheme.

Open blooms of *Rosa rugosa* 'Alba' with the yellow and white feverfew (*Tanacetum parthenium*).

Foxgloves over yellow Jerusalem sage (*Phlomis fruticosa*), with an early summer rose.

Color has been carefully managed in this garden. Yellow, white, and of course green, have been gathered together to create an informal planting area which remains restful.

Lilium 'Golden Splendor', adding a touch of the exotic to a white and yellow border. Lilies prefer full sun and free draining soil. Because of this they are often grown in pots.

White honesty, *Lunaria annua alba*, a biennial, with tulips in this display for spring.

White lilies stand out against the ice-blue eryngiums in this border.

165

Yellow with Red

Employ these strong colors together to create schemes which are hot, fiery and exciting. These are not shades to mix for those who like their gardens to be restful and easy on the eye. These are the colors to startle and surprise.

Setting is always important. A plain, dark background will set off these colors and avoid confusion where they mingle with paler shades.

This is a combination which is easy to achieve later in the year when the strong reds and yellows of heleniums mix with yellow rudbeckias and red echinaceas.

Lime-yellow bracts of *Euphorbia polychroma* with the dusky-red flowers of *Geum rivale* in early summer.

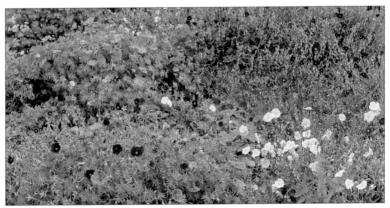

Orange, red and yellow helianthemums (rock roses) in early summer create a tapestry. The pinky-mauve cranesbills lead the eye away from the hot tones.

Mahogany-red *Helenium* 'Moerheim
Beauty' is toned down by creamy-yellow
Aconitum lycoctonum ssp. *vulparia*.

Lobelia 'Compliment Scarlet', over
Santolina chamaecyparissus 'Lemon Queen'
in a contrast of color and form.

With its soft, velvety foliage and creamy flowers *Verbascum nigrum* is the ideal
companion to this blood-red, late summer helenium for end of season excitement.

Yellow with Blue and Purple

Yellow with blue is a classic combination. Put with purple it is more unusual. The first is suggestive of the early part of the year. The second comes into its own as summer gathers pace. Yellow is a color to which the eye is automatically drawn. Linking it with another color, such as blue, reduces its force and, if lemon is used, brings it into the pastel range. With purple, gold and deep tones give a stronger impression, a heaviness even, which may require a lift with white, grey or silver.

A drift of Welsh poppies, *Meconopsis cambrica*, with forget-me-nots in this spring scheme.

Both these blue irises and yellow mimulus enjoy the moist soil on this bankside.

Yellow hemerocallis (day lilies) with china-blue cranesbill.

Buttermilk anthemis are complemented by scabious and phygelius.

Delphiniums are grown here with the pompon flowers of *Gentiana lutea*.

Pale mauve *Campanula lactiflora* is teamed with the homely yellow of *Verbascum nigrum*.

Scabious flowers contrast here with the flat heads of achillea.

In spring the Welsh poppy, *Meconopsis cambrica*, intermingles with bluebells, *Hyacinthoides non-scriptus*.

In this spring border the brightest yellow are the leaves of *Valeriana phu* 'Aurea'.

Borders like this one in spring have been planned with confidence. Color is restricted to blue and yellow, and plants are packed together for the greatest possible impact.

Violet-blue is accompanied by citrus yellow. Flowers in the foreground are *Asphodeline lutea*.

Coreopsis verticillata against which is grown the thistle heads of *Eryngium × zabelii*. Both plants are perennial and hardy.

Bold clumps of *Anthemis tinctoria* 'E.C. Buxton' are placed at regular intervals, whilst nepetas, salvias, and helianthus, yet to flower, are included not simply for color but for texture and form.

Blue with White

Together these colors make for cool schemes. This is a combination to follow an area of the garden which is devoted to warm shades. Most often the same flower is to be found in both blue and white, and effective schemes may be devised by using drifts of each in the same border. However, caution should be exercised in the positioning. Blue, unlike white, recedes and it is easy to finish up with an arrangement which is lacking in definition.

Rounded heads of border phlox are sharpened by the intense blue of the hardy agapanthus.

These white love-in-a-mist (*Nigella*) surround the palest of blue flowers of the *Polemonium* (Jacob's ladder).

The effect of mixing the same plant in different colors: blue and white *Campanula latifolia*.

Sweetly scented flowers of the Mexican orange blossom, *Choisya* 'Aztec Pearl', through which rise tall spires of blue camassia, *Camassia leichtlinii*, so that they become an integral part of the shrub.

White flowers of *Clematis montana* with mauve-blue *Abutilon* × *suntense* in the late spring.

Growing to 4 × 3in/10 × 7.5cm, *Anemone appenina* will produce flowers in springtime.

In the late spring. *Clematis montana* among the flowers of *Ceanothus* 'Blue Mound'. This clematis type is exceedingly vigorous and it is likely to choke the host shrub.

Although not strictly blue, the flowers of the violet, *Viola cornuta*, make a lovely contrast with the taller growing, white flowers of *Malva moschata alba*.

Ice-white bells of *Campanula persicifolia* are placed here with the yellow flowers of a perennial potentilla.

Eryngiums with white eschscholtzia, an annual which will flower summer to fall.

Lavender with Pinks and Reds

Misty lavender-blues combine with quiet pinks and rich reds to produce borders of pensive beauty through summer months. They are a foil to harsh sunlight and glare. Such blues are non-assertive, lacking the intensity of a clear blue, conveying a sense of distance. They blend with muted pinks and reds to resemble slightly faded damasks. These colors are the familiar mainstay of the garden, in possession of an unassuming elegance.

Universal pansies, 'True Blue', are placed amongst random drifts of the colorful daisy, *Bellis* 'Medicis', to create an arresting yet utterly pleasing combination.

Here the violet–blue flowers of *Campanula lactiflora* tone with the Gallica rose, *Rosa* 'Président de Sèze'.

Purple flowers of *Stachys macrantha* 'Robusta' harmonize with *Campanula lactiflora* 'Telham Beauty'.

Violet-crimson flowers of the rambling *Rosa* 'Bleu Magenta' pick up the veining of the geranium.

Rosa gallica officinalis, the red rose of Lancaster, plays host to *Clematis integrifolia*.

Velvet-red *Clematis viticella* 'Madame Julia Correvon' with *Clematis viticella* 'Venosa Violacea' in late summer.

The magenta *Lychnis coronaria* against the purple of a summer-flowering buddleja.

A composition for the early summer of plantings of pale pink roses and hardy geraniums. Plant varieties have been deliberately kept to a few, and all within a color range.

Violas and lamium in pink, mauve and lavender at the front of an herbaceous border.

Clematis montana 'Tetrarose' climbs through the long racemes of *Wisteria floribunda* during late spring.

Deep claret orach, *Atriplex hortensis* var. *rubra*, is a foil in this setting to the pale pink cranesbill.

A *Geranium cinereum* 'Ballerina', a lavender and white viola and summer-flowering diascias.

179

Massed Color

Massed schemes, perhaps because they bring to mind municipal parks and gardens, are somehow associated with bright, occasionally vulgar, effects. This need not be the case, and quieter plantings should not be overlooked. When massing any kind of color, be bold and decisive. Skimping on plants will result in an arrangement that looks thin, half-hearted and lacking in confidence. Too many colors will suggest uncertainty and will be in danger of losing direction. Remember, it is most often the simplest of ideas that work the best.

Bulbs are, of course, a particularly good way to achieve a massed display. Where change is required, then they may be interplanted with something different at the start of each new season.

Ribbons of color make for a different way of displaying spring favorites. Here the main components are *Tulipa* 'Golden Melody', wallflowers, 'Scarlet Bedding' and Universal pansies.

Bulbs have been set in such a way as to thrust their way through other spring bedding. Here buttery-yellow wallflowers, which must be set out in the previous fall, contrast with the tulip flowers.

A simple use of tulips which are allowed to drift through this border. The underplanting of forget-me-nots lifts the deep color of the bulbs and gives to the whole scheme a lightness and airiness.

This somewhat eclectic mix of rock roses, cranesbill and pansies are, in fact, in harmony.

Old-fashioned favorites, such as pansies and the hardy geraniums give a feeling of a cottage garden.

Had these geraniums and helianthemums been planted singly, then little impression would have been made. As it is, planted in the company of others, the overall effect is of one body of color.

Spires of *Verbena bonariensis* soar over deep pink *Salvia viridis*.

Annual marguerites and fuchsias make a display which should be long lasting.

Roses and peonies, two of the most splendid of all garden plants, convey a sense of luxury to any border. Together they give a wonderfully rich display in early summer.

Color in the Border

Borders without color would, it has to be admitted, be rather dull. After all, one of the principal delights of gardening has to be the arrangement of harmonious living pictures which will give satisfaction and be pleasing to the eye for as long a period as possible. That said, the organization of color is not straightforward. Plants, as we all know only too well, are fickle. Invariably they fail to grow exactly as expected, or, most likely, prove reluctant to flower at the very moment that is absolutely essential to the whole border composition.

Such pitfalls are not easily overcome and much will depend on trial and error, learning to work with your conditions, knowing your plants, resolving mistakes and building on successes.

Limiting the color range is often one way of bringing about a pleasing result. That is not to say your borders have to be of a single color. Rather, select plants which will flower within a controlled range, perhaps employing a variety of shades and tints which are based on two or three main colors.

Rose, pink, magenta, a touch of violet, bronze, these colors, all within the same range, contribute a sense of unity to this mainly herbaceous border.

A huge yew buttress makes a splendid background to this border which comprises perennials.

Purple-leafed foliage at either end of the border serves to create balance.

White achillea is used here to punctuate this border of deep pink and purple. Much thought has been given to the grouping to produce a gently undulating effect.

Note the way in which *Gladiolus communis byzantinus* has been placed as a ribbon of color.

Excellent use of soft yellow, found in the lupins and irises, and white.

Plants in profusion in complementary colors are the mark of this border seen at the start of summer.

Midsummer, and this border is seen at its best. Purple headed alliums, heleniums, phlox and coreopsis are all planted in generous clumps to give a furnished look.

Late summer lavender–mauve, deep pink and purple using asters, cone flowers (*Echinacea purpurea*) and *Verbena bonariensis*.

Fall Colors

The dying days of the gardening
year produce some of its richest
coloring. With certain plants this is
their greatest season, but there are
also many which reward with a final
display after earning their keep in
spring and summer.

Fall Foliage

Fall color on a grand scale is difficult to achieve in a garden setting and, never more so, where space is restricted. But this does not mean that spectacular effects cannot be achieved. By choosing trees and shrubs with care, and selecting those which will perform well in other seasons too, it is perfectly possible to bring to the smallest of gardens much of the drama which is so typical of this time of year. Among those to consider are birches, cherries, maples, rowans, sumachs and whitebeams as well as colorful dogwoods and the spindle berries.

What of course cannot be ignored is the difficulty of managing late color in the garden. As the year progresses, and the fall hues gather force, so summer color is becoming fast spent and it is too often against a background of dead and decaying perennials that these flashes of brilliance and glory are to be enjoyed. Try, therefore, to position your end-of-season display in such a way as it may be viewed without other distractions. If this is not totally possible, then a little timely cutting back and clearing will help matters considerably.

Pseudolarix amabilis For beauty and hardiness, and where space is not a problem, grow the golden larch. As fall approaches so leaves turn yellow. 52 × 52ft/18 × 18m

Betula pendula Silver birch is suitable for sunny or shady conditions. Spring catkins and yellow fall foliage make this a tree for all seasons. 33 × 25ft/10 × 7.5m

Acer campestre Easy and hardy, this acer is best reserved for the wild garden. In a more restricted area, select one of many smaller growing varieties offered by nurseries. 33 × 26ft/10 × 8m

Larix decidua The common larch is a vigorous, deciduous tree, suitable for most soils except very wet or dry, shallow chalk. Larch is a woodland tree making it inappropriate for a normal garden. 66 × 49ft/20 × 15m

Sorbus alnifolia Heavily veined burnt copper leaves at the close of the season. 33 × 33ft/10 × 10m

Nyssa sylvatica The Tupelo has spectacular fall foliage. For sun, moist soil. 52 × 39ft/16 × 12m

Cercidiphyllum japonicum The seasonal display compensates for insignificant flowers earlier on. 49 × 39ft/15 × 12m

***Acer japonicum* 'Vitifolium'** This shrub, a Japanese maple, has fan-shaped leaves. 15 × 15ft/4.5 × 4.5m

Acer obtusatum A maple whose leaves turn a fiery red in the later part of the year. 49 × 16ft/15 × 5m

Liquidamber styraciflua Unsuitable for shallow chalk, liquidamber prefers moist, well drained soil. 52 × 26ft/16 × 8m

Acer palmatum atropurpureum One of the most beautiful of maples. Finely cut leaves and graceful arching stems never appear out of place. 15 × 15ft/4.5 × 4.5m

***Prunus* × *yedoensis* 'Yoshino'** The spreading branches of the Yoshino Cherry carry white flowers in the early spring to be followed by bronze-orange foliage at the year's end. 26 × 26ft/8 × 8m

***Acer palmatum* 'Senkaki'** The Coral Bark Maple has coral-red branches, effective in winter. 15 × 15ft/4.5 × 4.5m

Acer palmatum Japanese maples have outstanding fall color. 15 × 15ft/ 4.5 × 4.5m

Sorbus sargentiana Of rigidly branched habit, this rowan with red leaf stalks colors vividly in the fall, topped by large rounded heads of small scarlet fruits. 26 × 26ft/ 8 × 8m

Enkianthus perulatus White flowers in spring, but it is the fall color which makes this such a desirable plant. Must be grown on neutral or acidic soil. 10 × 10ft/3 × 3m

Disanthus cercidifolius Few shrubs can rival this excellent specimen for its range of fall colors. An acid lover, this shrub should be planted in free-draining soil.
10 × 10ft/3 × 3m

Viburnum plicatum 'Mariesii' This shrub requires sufficient space to show itself off. Huge white flowers produce an abundant spring display. Easy. 10 × 10ft/3 × 3m

197

Euonymus alatus Dull, bronzy-green leaves turn to flame on this slow shrub. 10 × 10ft/3 × 3m

Viburnum recognitum This variety has yellow foliage at turn of year. 10 × 10ft/3 × 3m

Rhus typhina The staghorn sumach is renowned for its shape as well as its color at the close of the year. Erect seed heads continue through the winter. 16 × 20ft/5 × 6m

Fothergilla major Fragrant white flowers in spring and fall color. Slow growing, best planted in moist, acidic soil. 10 × 10ft/3 × 3m

Cercis canadensis **'Forest Pansy'** A slow growing form. 33 × 33ft/10 × 10m

Roga rugosa **'Alba'** In the fall they carry scarlet hips. 5 × 5ft/1.5 × 1.5m

Parthenocissus quinquefolia The Virginia creeper, self-clinging, is capable of covering an entire house with its deeply cut leaves which redden as the year advances. 39ft/12m

Cotoneaster horizontalis Throughout the period small red berries add decoration, unless raided by birds. It is possible to train this particular form against a wall.
6 × 6ft/2 × 2m

CONSIDER ALSO:

TREES:
*Crataegus ×
   prunifolia*

SHRUBS:
Cotinus coggygria
   'Royal Purple'

CLIMBERS:
*Parthenocissus
   henryana*
Vitis coignetiae
Vitis vinifera
   'Brandt'

***Berberis thunbergii* 'Atropurpurea'**
Decked with long-lasting scarlet berries.
6 × 6ft/2 × 2m

Fruits and Berries

Showy fruits and berries are, in the main, one of the delights of the fall. Appearing at the same time as brilliantly colored leaves, they add an additional sparkle and interest to trees and shrubs in the closing days of the year. But whereas fading foliage, however magnificent, is representative of decay and, of course, death, seasonal fruits are the culmination of nature's cycle and are a symbol of ripeness and richness.

Clinging on, as they so often do, into the depths of winter, until ravaged by hungry birds, fruits and berries take on a new lease of life when masked in hoar frost or lightly dusted with a coating of fresh snow. Then they become an exciting and integral part of a winter landscape which, in its own way, is as varied and interesting as that which is enjoyed during the long days of summer.

Cotoneaster frigidus **'Cornubia'** This hybrid is noted for its scarlet berries. Where cream and yellow fruits are preferred, then grow the form *Cotoneaster frigidus* 'Fructu Luteo'. 23 × 23ft/7 × 7m

Viburnum opulus 'Xanthocarpum'
Early fall berries ripen on this shrub.
15 × 15ft/4.5 × 4.5m

Malus × zumi 'Golden Hornet' From
late summer well into winter golden crabs
crowd this small tree. 13 × 20ft/4 × 6m

Sorbus 'Joseph Rock' Mountain ashes
are easily accommodated in gardens.
39 × 23ft/12 × 7m

Cotoneaster salicifolius 'Exburyensis' An
excellent, evergreen shrub which is well
worth seeking out. 16 × 16ft/5 × 5m

Sorbus vilmorinii After the flowers these pale pink berries appear. 16 × 16ft/ 5 × 5m

***Sorbus cashmiriana* 'Rosiness'** A small tree which may be grown as a shrub. 16 × 16ft/5 × 5m

Sorbus sargentiana These berries of late summer, provide rich color. 16 × 16ft/ 5 × 5m

***Sorbus* 'Winter Cheer'** The berries of this mountain ash will last. 39 × 23ft/12 × 7m

Malus × *robusta* '**Red Sentinel**' As the leaves of this small crab fall, so these apples are revealed which are ignored by birds at least until the worst of winter. 13 × 20ft/ 4 × 6m

Viburnum betulifolium White flowers of summer, scarlet berries of fall.
15 × 15ft/4.5 × 4.5m

Viburnum opulus The guelder rose. White flowers early summer, then berries.
15 × 15ft/4.5 × 4.5m

***Rosa moyesii* 'Geranium'** Blood-red flowers of the early summer are followed later on with these heps which decorate the stems throughout fall. 8 × 7ft/2.4 × 2.2m

Cornus kousa The Chinese dogwood is a
shrub with white flowers in summer.
12 × 13ft/3.6 × 4m

Berberis thunbergii As the fall approaches
stems are lined with red berries.
4 × 4ft/1.2 × 1.2m

Of all berrying shrubs, pyracanthas are amongst the most distinctive. Wall-trained, they
bring life to shady sides of a house.

Arbutus unedo The Killarney strawberry tree will tolerate some lime. E, 16 × 16ft/ 5 × 5m

Photinia davidiana A shrub which bears bunches of berries. E, 20 × 13ft/ 6 × 4m

Hypericum × inodorum **'Elstead'** These plants are prone to rust in most gardens. 4 × 4ft/1.2 × 1.2m

Euonymus europaeus Perfectly happy on chalk, the spindle tree is alight in fall. A named variety to look out for is *Euonymus europaeus* 'Red Cascade'. 15 × 15ft/ 4.5 × 4.5m

Euonymus cornutus var. *quinquecornutus* Evergreen in mild areas, this shrub is adorned in the fall with extraordinary berries. 6 × 6ft/2 × 2m

Callicarpa bodinieri **var.** *geraldii* This shrub turns purple and produces remarkable berries. 13 × 13ft/4 × 4m

Pernettya (Gaultheria) mucronata Shrub will produce berries of white, pink, red, purple or black. Acid soil.
◐, E, 2.5 × 4ft/75cm × 1.2m

Of all garden shrubs, cotoneasters are hardy, quick-growing and easy in cultivation thriving on most fertile soils providing that they are fairly free draining.

***Arum italicum* 'Pictum'** As the marbled leaves of this perennial disappear, it berries. ●, 10 × 8in/25 × 20cm

Iris foetidissima Seed pods of the Gladwin iris burst open in winter. E, 1.5 × 2ft/45 × 60cm

Skimmia japonica To effect pollination of skimmias, plant male and female varieties together. There is a so-called hermaphrodite cultivar, *Skimmia japonica* 'Veitchii'. All will succeed in partial or complete shade.

Bark and Stems

At their most striking in wintertime, trees, free of the distraction of leaf cover, make an exciting contribution to the garden scene.

At this period it is, of course, the color of bark which is likely to be noticed. But also its richness of color, pattern and textural quality which is particularly welcome out of season.

Acer griseum The paperbark maple. Fall leaves are red and gold. 26 × 20ft/8 × 6m

Eucalyptus pauciflora **ssp.** *niphophila*
Plant in a position out of reach of cold winds. ○, E, 33 × 26ft/10 × 8m

Cornus alba Grow this easy shrub for its stems which light up a winter border. 10 × 10ft/3 × 3m

Salix alba vitellina **'Britzensis'** Treat this shrubby willow to the same hard pruning as for Cornus alba. 10 × 10ft/3 × 3m

Cornus stolonifera **'Flaviramea'** All winter the stems of this dogwood contribute color. In summer small white flowers are produced, but these lack any significance. 6 × 12ft/2 × 4m

Stuartia sinensis Plant in a lightly shaded spot in moist soil rich in humus.
15 × 15ft/4.5 × 4.5m

Acer capillipes One of the snake bark maples noted for the white stripes down the bark. 33 × 26ft/10 × 8m

Prunus serrula Rich mahogany bark of this cherry polished by winter sunshine.
30 × 30ft/9 × 9m

Betula ermanii This is a tree for the border or as a lawn specimen. 49 × 15ft/15 × 4.5m

Betula utilis* var. *jacquemontii The trunk of this specimen tree stands out even when cloaked in leaves. In fall foliage turns golden. 49 × 16ft/15 × 5m

Color Around the Garden

Color need not be restricted to beds and borders and their grand set-piece displays when warmer days arrive. There are many ways for a gardener to bring color to other areas.

Alpine and Rock Garden

Most alpine and rock plants require good drainage. They much prefer to be planted in a gritty medium through which water will readily run. For many, the worst of the winter weather is nothing to being water-logged or to having water, even ice, collecting around the crown. Many, but by no means all, enjoy the warmth of the sun, something to bear in mind when establishing a new rock garden.

A visit to an alpine nursery will give a good indication of just how many rock plants there are. Choose from minute columbines, like the violet-blue *Aquilegia bertolonii*, miniature pinks like *Dianthus* 'Inshriach Dazzler' or *Dianthus* 'La Bourboule', even a miniature cotton lavender, *Santolina elegans*. The list is endless and, ultimately, choice will reflect personal taste.

A colorful mixture of rock plants. In this garden the plan has clearly been to create a tapestry of color rather than to consider a more limited, restricted scheme. A path allows for inspection of the plants.

Fritillaria pyrenaica From the Pyrenees, and known as the Pyrenean snakeshead, this bulb produces these lovely flower heads of dusky purple, checkered with yellow, in the spring of each year. 1ft/30cm

Pulsatilla vulgaris rubra Flowering at Easter, this is a long-lived perennial. 1 × 1ft/30 × 30cm

Pulsatilla vulgaris Normally deep purple, this form is of a pale lilac. 1 × 1ft/ 30 × 30cm

Sempervivums, or house leeks, make splendid subjects with which to fill containers.

Erinus alpinus A short lived perennial. Pink flowers in early summer. ◯, E, 1–2in/2.5–5cm

Ajuga reptans **'Pink Surprise'** A form of bugle. Foliage is evergreen. 6in × 2ft/ 15 × 60cm

Purple aubrieta and yellow alyssum. Cut back hard once the flowering is over.

***Dianthus* 'Gravetye Gem'** Old-fashioned pinks are one of the delights of the garden in summer not only for their pretty flowers but also for their heavenly scent. ○, E, 6in × 1ft/15 × 30cm

***Lamium maculatum* 'Wootton Pink'** A dead nettle which is not invasive. Flowers in summer. 6in × 1ft/15 × 30cm

Diascia cordata Flowers of this small perennial are produced throughout the summer. 8 × 8in/20 × 20cm

Herb and Kitchen Garden

All too often the herb and kitchen gardens are considered purely as functional. True, it has to be said, in recent times there has been a revival of interest in creating formally designed herb gardens where the emphasis is firmly placed on pattern, color and form rather than to serve any serious domestic purpose. In small gardens, where space is at a premium, then herbs are often included for their ornamental value in the mixed border.

The same cannot, sadly, be said of vegetables. In too many cases there is a reluctance to grow these other than for their primary purpose, to be eaten. The imaginative gardener will naturally recognize the merits of many vegetables and will wish to include them, not least for their color, as part of general border schemes.

Summer flowering roses, which may be picked for the house, are central to this formally designed herb garden where sage, rosemary and chives, for kitchen use, are included.

This French *Lavandula stoechas* is combined here with a pale pink bistort, *Polygonum bistorta*.

This highly ornate corner of a garden demonstrates how a working area can be integrated.

Rows of chard, beetroot and lettuce have been interplanted with nasturtiums.

Yellow evening primrose and lavender with the green leaves of spearmint.

Traditional herb gardens more often than not are based on a formal design in which beds, based on squares and rectangles, are divided by low box hedging.

The onions contained within this box edged bed are arranged to be decorative.

Wavy asparagus foliage provides variation in form and texture to the lettuces.

Runner beans could well be sited at the back of a mixed border.

Color and form. Here chives and mint jostle with each other for attention.

The Water Garden

You may, if you are very fortunate indeed, be in the enviable position of having natural water, in the form of a stream or a pond, within your garden. Most people, though, have to rely on something which is artificially created and whilst this in itself is not a problem, disguising the installation often is.

It may well be that the best policy is to select plants which will perform well together in a particular season, say spring, and accept that this is the time of year when the water garden will be at its best. For the rest of the year the emphasis will be on maintaining a tidy appearance with, perhaps, the inclusion of a massed, block planting of a single perennial to give flower color at another time. Planning color in this way will, except when working on a large scale, give very much more satisfying results.

These candelabra primula make a statement of color. Contrast is brought about with yellow flag irises and golden sedge, the whole planned for the early summer.

Primula sieboldii This variety of primula flowers in spring in a cool, moist situation. By midsummer it will have died down. 6 × 6in/15 × 15cm

Primula pulverulenta A form of candelabra primula in early summer. 2 × 1ft/60 × 30cm

Of all aquatic plants, that is to say those which grow in water, water lilies remain favorite.

227

Caltha palustris **'Flore Pleno'** Spring color with this perennial marsh marigold. 1 × 1ft/30 × 30cm

Primula florindae Bells during summer. Some shade during the day. 2.5 × 2.5ft/ 75 × 75cm

Lysichiton americanus These spathes appear in the spring before leaves develop. 3 × 2.5ft/1m × 75cm

Lysichiton camtschatcensis A white skunk cabbage which is smaller in habit. 2.5 × 2ft/75 × 60cm

Geum rivale **'Leonard's Variety'** The perennial water avens, flowering in spring. 1.5 × 1.5ft/45 × 45cm

Astilbe **'Erica'** All of the summer-flowering astilbes carry these plumes. 3 × 3ft/1 × 1m

Mimulus **'Orange Glow'** This summer perennial is an unusual variety. All mimulus should be planted in moisture retentive soil. 2 × 2ft/60 × 60cm

The Winter Garden

Winter is not, as everyone knows, a season of extravagant color. And yet it is not without interest. Trees and shrubs, laid bare, reveal their structure and form, vistas, which remain closed in summer, are opened to view.

But it is the flowers in the borders which attract most attention and which give so much pleasure. Here are to be found the earliest of the bulbs – aconites, crocuses and, of course, snowdrops. To these may be added miniature irises and those most wonderful of early flowering perennials, hellebores. Among these, before the *Helleborus orientalis* forms, are those like the Christmas rose (*Helleborus niger*), red stemmed *Helleborus foetidus* 'Wester Flisk' and the beautiful *Helleborus lividus*. Add to this flowering shrubs, colored conifers, and even a clematis or two, and the picture is very much alive.

Here large evergreen and ruby colored conifers have been planted with sweeps of winter-flowering heather, *Erica carnea*, in a broad island bed to give a vibrant display of color.

Iris unguicularis Algerian iris. Ideally, plant in poor soil against a hot, dry wall. E, 8in × 2ft/20 × 60cm

Cyclamen coum Allow hardy cyclamen to colonize underneath deciduous trees. 4in/10cm

Iris reticulata **'Harmony'** To increase, propagate by division during late summer. ○, 4–6in/10–15cm

Galanthus nivalis Position in some shade and divide immediately flowers have gone over. 6 × 6in/15 × 15cm

Eranthis hyemalis Winter aconite flourish in humus-rich soil in semi-shade. 4 × 6in/10 × 15cm

Jasminum nudiflorum This shrub may be trained against a wall or to cover a fence. 10ft/3m

Hamamelis mollis Include this shrub as a centerpiece to the winter border. Witch hazels are slow growing and will take many years before they fill their space. 8 × 10ft/ 2.4 × 3m

Clematis cirrhosa Early evergreen clematis. Afford it shelter. E, 6 × 3ft/ 2 × 1m

Narcissus bulbocodium Planted deeply, these will flower year after year. ◑, 6 × 8in/15 × 20cm

Helleborus lividus The leaves of this hellebore are attractive all year round. Not the hardiest of hellebores so give a sheltered position. E, ◑, 1.5 × 1.5ft/45 × 45cm

Color in the Conservatory

If you are fortunate enough to own a conservatory, or to have a greenhouse in the garden which you are able to keep free of frost, then you will be able to enjoy year-round color, even at a time when there is little in flower outside. A visit to a good florist or garden center should prove to be a most rewarding experience and you will doubtless find yourself spoilt for choice.

But a conservatory does not necessarily have to be entirely for decoration. Any heated space can be utilized as a home for tender perennials which will not overwinter outside or a space in which to keep cuttings of half-hardy favorites.

Do remember that all indoor plants require regular watering and feeding. This is particularly so during the summer months.

Jasminum polyanthum Of immense value in a cool conservatory, this loveliest jasmine will flood fragrance from flowers in late spring. ○, E, 15ft/5m

Anisodontea capensis This sub-shrub will flower all summer and winter too under glass. ○, 3 × 3ft/1 × 1m

Fuchsia Grow them for their brilliant flower from early summer onwards.

Brugmansia (Datura) Angel's trumpets flower during the summer. 4 × 3ft/ 1.2 × 1m

Geraniums are used widely. This is *Pelargonium* 'Madame Layal'.

Thunbergia alata Black-eyed Susan, an easily grown climber in flower for summer. ○, 6ft/2m

Euryops pectinatus A small shrub smothered in daisy flowers. 2 × 2ft/ 60 × 60cm

Clivia miniata Flowers are borne over a long period. In containers this makes a spectacular plant. 2 × 1ft/60 × 30cm

Nerium oleander Best placed outside in summer and returned for winter. 4 × 3ft/1.2 × 1m

Plumbago capensis This climbing shrub flowers in late summer and early fall. 6ft/2m

Cymbidium ruspex **'Ivory Queen'** An orchid which may be grown successfully as a potted plant. 2 × 1ft/60 × 30cm

Pots and Containers

For those with very tiny or even no garden at all, pots are one way of creating color in a small space. In larger gardens they may be used to enliven dull spots in borders, as eye-catchers to close vistas, as pointers around the garden, to draw attention to a particular area or simply as decorative ornament. In every situation they may be employed to mark an entrance, such as either side of a doorway or positioned on gate piers, to furnish a terrace, patio or outside sitting or eating area, to line a pathway as a means of introducing a note of formality, or merely in a functional manner as a way of growing half hardy plants which will require winter protection.

Whatever, it must be remembered that pots and containers, once filled with soil and planted out, are permanently in need of care and attention. They must not be allowed to dry out. They will need feeding regularly throughout the season. Finally, attention to deadheading will encourage repeat flowers.

Displays of this kind can really only be effected with brightly colored annuals which, if not fully hardy, may not be put outside until all danger of frost has passed.

Hanging basket, crowded with fuchsia, petunia and lobelia, in a color theme.

A gorgeous array of color cleverly arranged in a single hanging basket.

Cheerful bedding plants join hands with the more somber, permanent ivy around this window to form an integrated summer display. The containers have been disguised by the massed planting.

Such a composition can be re-arranged in a moment as the mood takes you.

Setting these hot colors against a dark, evergreen background shows them to advantage.

The glowing acers are well matched to the dark pots which contain them.

Here the foliage of the agapanthus is as important as the flower.

A formal setting lends itself to containers like this classical urn. Filled with spring tulips and complementary pansies, they never appear out of place.

This pot contains *Fritillaria imperialis* surrounded by blood-red tulips.

These two Versailles planters contain box pyramids as permanent structure.

Pots where the flower color is severely restricted require the most confidence to create.

A sense of theatre in the placing of parrot tulips against this paintwork.

The formality of the trellis fence arranged in arches demands the kind of repeated planting which is shown here. The focal point of each planter is the box ball.

Huge box balls sit in these black painted planters to mark the approach.

Annual color is added to these pots to surround perennial plantings. In time the shrubs will grow.

243

Relying in the main on two flowering plants with complementary foliage gives satisfying unity.

This collection of spring flowers is a delightful way in which to end a path.

Planting is simple, the succulent chosen to pick up the color of the paintwork.

Flower is restricted to the skimmias with box and ivy retaining color all year.

Different plants with flowers from the same spectrum. Here the pinks tie in together.

An old copper pot, splendidly planted, is placed in the middle of a crossing point of two paths.

A charming mixture for the early spring gives the effect of a cottage garden in miniature.

A happy mixture in this collection which is sited on the treads of these steps.

Acknowledgements

Many of the photographs were taken in the author's garden, Arrow Cottage, Ledgemoor, Weobley, England. The publishers would also like to thank the many people and organizations in the United Kingdom. whose gardens have appeared in this book, including the following:

Acton Beauchamp Roses, Worcester; Mr and Mrs A. Bambridge, Llanvair Kilgeddin, Abergavenny; Barnsley House, Barnsley, Cirencester; Burford House, Tenbury Wells; Chilcombe House, Chilcombe, Dorset; Dr A. and Dr L. Cox, Woodpeckers, Marlcliff, Bidford-on-Avon; Richard Edwards, Well Cottage, Blakemere; The Hon Mrs Peter Healing, The Priory, Kemerton; Hergest Croft, Kington; Kiftsgate Court, near Chipping Campden; Mr and Mrs D. Lewis, Ash Farm, Much Birch; Oxford Botanic Gardens; Mrs Richard Paice, Bourton House Garden, Bourton-on-the-Hill, Moreton-in-Marsh; Parham House, Parham; The Picton Garden, Colwall; Anthony Poulton, 21 Swinton Lane, Worcester; Powis Castle (National Trust); Royal Botanic Gardens, Kew; RHS Garden, Wisley; The Weir, Swainshill, Hereford (National Trust); Wakehurst Place (National Trust).

Index